A ROYAL PULPIT

FIFTY YEARS OF PREACHING
IN THE CLASSIC TRADITION

MICHAEL EDWARD ELLIS, DMIN
PASTOR, EDUCATOR, PRESIDING ELDER

Inquiries and Book Orders should be addressed to:

Great Writers Media
Email: info@greatwritersmedia.com
Phone: 877-600-5469

ISBN: 978-1-960939-15-9 (sc)
ISBN: 978-1-960939-16-6 (ebk)

CONTENTS

———— ∝ ————

FOREWORD

—————⧓—————

At this particular point in the midlife or autumn of my life, though a diary was not kept, I can recall most of the people, places, and events that made my life at least worthy of talking about. I understand fully that every detail of my past life was an integral part of the preparation for my future. This religious journey into the vast areas of my life focuses on selective particulars of my personal experiences and the application of my biblical studies, preaching, and teaching. Looking back at my past has helped me to tell others about life changes and about God.

So what am I to make of this heritage? What's the influence of the gene pool that has swirled in my bloodstream for more than fifty years? One could accept this curious arrangement that we call preaching if he could honestly assign to the preacher any esoteric knowledge of the ways of God with man or man with God. The preacher may or may not have specialized training in the theological disciplines, but these are areas that can scarcely claim to do more than to deal with observable explanations and interpretations of vital religious experience. They can hardly plead that they are of a level with what is meant by "I know whom I have believed."

The Drew University school of Divinity has a motto that is written on the walls in the entrance of the beautiful campus that says, **"Freely ye have received, freely give"** (Matthew 10:8) (KJV). As much as men are able to appropriate the divine mind, the humblest layperson has the same access as the man or woman whose vocation is that of a preacher. The preacher does not enjoy the right to any esoteric knowledge of God denied to those to whom one preaches.

The role of the preacher would be more reasonable to the mind if they who preach could assert truthfully that they enjoy by virtue of their office as preacher a moral superiority over those to whom they address the gospel.

The magnificent anomaly of preaching is to be found in the fact that the person who preaches is in need of the message that he or she is ordained to utter. How dare such a person address others, in the name of God, who are no worse off than the spokesman! The word that the preacher is called to speak is rough with the harshness of judgment in it, sweeping, devastating. He is called on, also, to speak of God's mercy, and this may be more painful to those to whom it is proclaimed than is the judgment of God.

ACKNOWLEDGEMENTS

———— ⟨⟩ ————

I am deeply grateful to have lived my life around so many wonderful people. These are the people who had an indomitable influence in my life and ministry. I feel a deep sense of gratitude for my parents, who guided me in the way I should go; I know their prayers and thoughts helped to make me who I am today. I never really thought about reaching this milestone of fifty years in the ministry, but by God's grace and mercy, here I am—blessed, humbled, grateful to Almighty God for allowing me these years of service to Him and the kingdom. Ever since I was a little boy, I have always wanted to preach. Someone close to me said, "It's your birthmark." I don't know about that, but this is the profession, the vocation or, more realistically, the calling I had on my life, and to be here at this moment to celebrate with family, friends, colleagues, classmates, this "milestone" is enriching to me personally, and humbling to my ministry. You can't get this far in your life's work or service without realizing how God has made a way for you and how much love and support from family, friends, and colleagues has supported you.

I am deeply grateful for the family I was born into—a nurturing mother, the late Mrs. Gwendolyn Ruth Turner Ellis, and a supportive father, the late Mr. George Henry Ellis—for all their love and prayers in my early life to my manhood. I enjoyed the interaction with my siblings: Arthur "A.T." Turner, Calvin Turner, George Collins Ellis, Gwendolyn Nancy Ellis Hall, Wayne Richard Ellis, and Brenda Jean Ellis Chalk. They were there for my first sermon and continue to be there to this day.

I am pleased to have been mentored and inspired from the Episcopacy of our church by none other than the late Bishop Raymond Luther Jones and the late Mrs. Mabel Miller Jones, who were very influential in guiding me as a young preacher in the church and who didn't mind taking me on Bishop Jones's Episcopal visits where I heard him preach masterful sermons with great power.

I am deeply grateful for the warm bond and friendship of more than thirty years with Rev. Dr. Joel D. Miles and his wife, Rev. Ruby D. Miles. A friendship that began in Knoxville, Tennessee, where we pastored together and lived next door to one another.

My immediate past bishop and supervisor, Bishop and Mrs. George W. C. Walker Sr. for appointing me the pastor of Columbus Avenue A.M. E. Zion Church, Boston, MA, and the presiding elder of the Greensboro District. I served with him for more than eighteen years, and the work and friendship continues to this day.

My present bishop and supervisor, Bishop and Mrs. George Edward Battle Jr., are an asset in my life and ministry. I have been blessed to serve with this wonderful team for many years, and his leadership and friendship is a model of what ministry is all about.

My ministry was blessed at the beginning because of the stellar and loving leadership of Rev. Dr. Vernon A. Shannon, who was my pastor at Moore's Chapel A.M.E. Zion Church, in Salisbury, NC. Rev. Shannon nurtured me as a "boy preacher" and allowed me to grow under his leadership. I was one of the first acolytes to serve at Moore's Chapel and he was instrumental in starting a club called the Crusader's Club for young men interested in the ministry. He is indeed "My Father in the Ministry" and I'm honored that he, along with his wife, Mrs. Mildred Shannon, took the time to nurture and encourage me.

I also wish to thank the Rev. Dr. W. Robert Johnson III, who served as my pastor and was very supportive in my first appointment at Liberty A.M.E. Zion Church. He encouraged me and had a listening ear when I needed someone to talk to. I want to also thank the late Rev. and Mrs. N. K. Byers, my first presiding elder of the Salisbury District. He allowed me every opportunity to preach on the district, which gave me invaluable experience.

I owe a debt of gratitude to my loving wife, Renee, who has stood by my side these twenty-eight years. She has been my "princess" and friend who prays for me daily. She encouraged me to write a book, and by God's grace it has become a reality.

Finally, I am grateful for a wonderful son, Michael II, and my daughter, Zoya, whose presence and prayers have been my deepest pleasure, and because of them in my life, I am striving to be a model father and role model in their lives. My granddaughter, McKenzie, is growing daily and is my pride. She is quite a little lady who is making me proud to be her grandfather; you might even say she's the "apple of my eye."

INTRODUCTION

———— ∝ ————

T he Royalty of the Pulpit is a unique nature of the Christian pulpit, the halo of majesty, romance, and noble traditions that crowns the preacher's high calling and mission. These fifty years have given me a picture of the ideal and inspiration that comes when one mounts the pulpit to declare the word of God. Practically every phase of the ministerial vocation is given adequate treatment: pulpit and pastoral responsibilities; churchmanship; and the myriad aspects of the preacher's relationship to his church, his study, and the community. God may use special events to direct a call to someone.

In fact, all events in people's lives are special events if they will see them as that. Browning wrote these words: "Earth's crammed with heaven." What he was saying is these happenings determine who we are and what direction we take. They determine further whether or not we have a sense of vocation or a sense of the call to ministry or to whatever we do. It is interesting that in the Gospel of John, it is said that when some people heard the voice of God, they thought it was thunder. So they missed the profound impact. They did not discern His voice, but Jesus did. It was available to all who were present, but they were not available to it.

Many probably believe that this kind of supernatural sign does not occur today. I think everything has a stamp of the supernatural that is evident to those who can recognize it. A person's previous life is not determinative in regard to ministry. Ultimately, this is a mystery, and we have to treat it as such. Yet there is something in us that longs for explanation and for rationalization, but much of God's calling cannot be subjected to analysis.

The gospel calls us to a stance, a position that is beyond immediate cultural background. One is the reflection of the changing world that it gives. In my fifty years of preaching I have seen and experienced tremendous change in many realms of thought.. These sermons register the trends, the changes in mood, the emergence of new interests, the bewildering onrush of new problems.

It is inevitable that preaching, over such a span of years, should change. There is no need to reiterate here the oft-told tale of the changed conditions which the preaching of the Christian gospel has had to meet. But just mere listening to a few of the great issues confronting the Christian Church in these years will help us see the sermons more vividly in relation to their time.

This review of preaching during my fifty years in ministry will stir the wonder about the future of preaching. The Royalty of the Pulpit deepens the conviction that amid the many changes, as long as human nature remains the same, the communication of thought and feeling and faith will be a high and permanent experience of humankind.

Of all the professions for young men and women to look forward to, I do not know of another one that seems to have such scope before it in the future as preaching.

SERMONS ON THE CHRISTIAN LIFE

---———— ⊱ ————---

The soul that rises with us, our life's star,
  Hath had elsewhere its setting
And cometh from afar;
Not in entire forgetfulness
But trailing clouds of glory do we come
From God who is our home.

—William Wordsworth

O ur lives run from God, in God, to God again. And all the time we are on earth there is stamped on every soul the three words "Made in Heaven." All of which is to say that if God sees all our dirty little secrets and still wishes us well, loves us warts and all, then we should be able, with steadfast gaze, to examine ourselves without despair. We can live amid our earthly imperfections because we live in the fullness of Heaven.

If we didn't have so many faults, we wouldn't be so eager to find them in others. If we believe that we ourselves came to earth trailing clouds of glory from God, who is our home, then we see a derivative sanctity in everyone. The ancient Jews were careful never to walk on a piece of paper for fear the name of God might be written on it. We should be so careful not to tread on others. Life can be worth living if it is used, moved by God, dedicated to the glory of God and the sanctity of life. May the spirit help us through these messages to accept our acceptance.

FACING DIFFICULT SITUATIONS

———✠———

Titus 1:5 (KJV)

"For this cause left I thee in Crete, that thou shouldest set in order the things that are wanting."

This is Paul's letter to a young disciple named Titus. It is believed that Paul wrote this letter, although some scholars think that he did not. Paul had left Titus upon the great island of Crete in the Eastern Mediterranean, and this island of Crete was not at all a desirable place for a Christian to be left.

The situation is summarized in one verse of this letter. Paul says, one of their prophets said, "Cretans are liars, evil beast idle gluttons." This was no hearsay but words of truth. This is Paul's summary of the situation in Crete and of the character of its people. But listen to him as he writes to Titus, "For this cause left I thee in Crete, that shouldest set in order the things that are wanting." That is an unusual reason for leaving a man in Crete, that the Cretans are always liars, evil beasts, and gluttons. It sounds like a good reason for getting out of Crete. But Paul was a man of stern fiber. He himself never shrank, and he never wanted his followers to shrink from the challenge of a difficult situation. He felt the stimulus of a hostile environment. There is something profoundly characteristic of the man himself in that attitude. Put yourself in Titus's place as he received this letter. I surmise that it must have been a letter that Paul wrote to Titus in answer to one that he had received from him, and it ought not to be difficult to reconstruct the spirit in which Titus wrote:

Dear Paul, this is an awful place. The people are hopeless, and the poor, struggling Christian movement is only rags and tatters. I am remaining here until you say Go, but I can't get away fast enough. For pity's sake, don't make me stay here all winter. There isn't a decent chance.

Obediently but unhappily yours, Titus." And then he got this letter. *"Titus, said Paul in effect, you are right about the Cretans. They are liars, evil beasts, idle gluttons. There isn't anything too bad that you can say about them. Crete is in deep need.* Let us put ourselves in Titus's place. It ought not to be difficult. One way or another we are always getting into Crete. There are many differences that separate us here this morning, but any preacher could be sure of one thing that unites us. We all have been in Crete, we are going to be in Crete, probably most of us are in Crete now. We are human and complaining, and we want to get out of Crete. I wonder what Titus said to himself when he faced this stunning message, **"For this cause left I thee in Crete"**

First of all, one must learn to be productive in the situation.

Titus must have reminded himself of some simple but profound common-sense things about life that he ought never to have forgotten. I think he said to himself, "Paul is right. After all, happiness is not something you find. It is something you make. And if you start with that attitude you might just as well create happiness in Crete as anywhere else."

When a person lands in Crete as probably Titus did, hoping to find it a pleasant place, he is destined for disappointment. He walks up and down Crete looking for happiness, but it isn't to be found. The Cretans are a bad lot. Then he gets this message that changes his inner attitude. He walks up and down Crete now not looking for ready-made happiness but looking for an opportunity. He had been left in Crete to use it as so much raw material out of which to make something. He is saying to himself, "Life is not something that you find; life is something that you create." Crete did turn out to be one of the greatest opportunities that Christianity had in that ancient world. History says that there was some excavating of churches from the early days when the gospel went out against the paganism of the Roman Empire. Out of that came teachers, preachers, and missionaries of the church. Whose name is on those churches? Titus's! Whose shrines were built there? Titus's! Just think—in the very place from which once he could not soon enough get away! Paul was right. **"For this cause left I thee in Crete, that shouldest set in order the things that were wanting"**

I think this principle runs through all of life. Life is not what you find; it is what you create. People wander in the world and pick up everything they can get their hands on looking for life. They never get it. What they get is existence. Existence is what you find; life is what you create.

In Alex Haley's *Roots,* Kunta Kinte drove his master to a plantation ball. As Kunta Kinte relaxed in the carriage to wait for his master's return, he heard in the distance some sounds other than the white people's music. It was a different sound. His feet took him in the direction of the luring notes coming from the slaves' cabins. As he got closer, Kunta Kinte recognized the music to be that of his native African tribe. Upon entering the cabin, he found fellow slaves who had been taken from the same part of Africa as he. They conversed in their native tongues. They sang their native songs. They remembered their common heritage. Even though Kunta Kinte was in another country, it wasn't the best situation, but he found life when he remembered his roots and that life was not perfect, but he could create some happiness in what he found.

Another example is Paul, who was a seasoned handler of difficult situations. He wanted to go to Bithynia, but the spirit of God suffered him not and he ended up in Troas. But Troas opened a way for him to extend his ministry. Paul rendered his most significant service with the leftovers of a broken plan. All life must be tackled as Titus tackled Crete. Life had not been so good, but he took what he had and made something better.

Second, in the situation people find themselves in they must be persistent followers

Titus must have said, "Paul is right!" This principle he recommends is not only common sense; it is good Christianity. There is no use pretending to be disciples of Jesus if we are unwilling to stay in Crete because it is difficult. Jesus belongs in Crete! Jesus particularly belongs in Crete—not in spite of the fact that the Cretans are liars, beasts, gluttons but *because* they are. What did they say about Jesus? "This man receiveth sinners and eateth with them." He was always trying to discover Crete. "The publicans and sinners were drawing near unto him to hear him." He always attracted Crete to himself.

There is no use pretending to be a disciple if we are dodging Crete. Imagine the Master in some discouraged hour when things were going badly with his ministry saying, "O God, human beings are a cruel lot. They are selfish, sensual, hateful, and brutish. Already I can see what their fathers did to the prophets they are going to do to me. What voice would we have heard out of the unseen?" **"For this cause sent I thee into the world"** You cannot imagine the Master going into any situation without making it his first business to look up Crete. "They that are well have no need of a physician. I came not to call the righteous but sinners to repentance."

How often we respectable Christians have gone on building churches, worshiping through splendid rituals, but the real spirit of Jesus has been somewhere else. Wherever in this modern world, there is a Crete, where the situation is difficult and people needy, there is a real spirit of Jesus calling to us that "though he was rich, yet for your sakes he became poor, that ye through his poverty might become rich." When a person lives in the spirit of Jesus, it is more satisfying than anything one can think of. The deepest joy in life is to find an undeveloped situation, to see the possibilities, to get something done there that would not have been done except for our creative soul.

The joy of every preacher is not that he preaches to this number of people or that, but once in a while he comes within the reach of an individual who needs a word of encouragement. That's what the writers meant when they penned these words: **"If I can help somebody as I pass along, If I can cheer somebody with a word or song, If I can show somebody he is traveling wrong, then my living will not be in vain."**

Nothing is more satisfying than to discover a soul in Crete and lead it to Christ. Don't dodge Crete. If we are to be persistent Christians, then we are to do love's message in the human heart.

Third and finally, you must have the power to see it through.

One other thing I think Titus said when Paul's letter came. I suspect he thought to himself, "Paul was right." The ultimate test of a man's faith in God is its power to see him through a hard place. Crete was a hard place, so hard and the people so unlovely that I suspect moral indignation had a good deal to do with Titus's first attitude. It would have been such a relief to his sense to tell them what he thought of them—liars, beasts, gluttons—and then leave them so.

That's natural! Many of us here I suspect are tempted to deal with some situations that we face by that cheap and easy method of moral indignation. It is much easier to denounce than to build. When one is in Crete, it's easier to be indignant than to be constructive. It's easier to be critical than to be supportive. And Crete has a way of getting into our lives and we have a much deeper problem—the problem of keeping Crete from becoming our spiritual enemy rather than our spiritual friend. That is the hardest thing some of us have to do: to take a situation that we hate and say, "I'm not going to let you be my spiritual enemy. You are not going to scare me, intimidate me, or crush me." When life leads you by the emotions, you get nothing done. You must learn to make the powered thrust in your life work to handle the strain, handle the difficulties with thought, to get it done without breaking yourself. I think Titus must have learned that real strength in handling bad situations is knowing where to find power when we need it.

Wherever your Crete is, stay there and battle your way through and let God give you the nourishment to grow up to maturity—taking in the bitter and the sweet. You'll become a better person and you will discover God made you a winner! That might be the way for you to get to heaven. I'm told that the chicken comes into the world as an embryo wrapped in mucus in a darkened shell. But he keeps feasting on that mucus until one day the shell is dry. He's alive; he's strong enough and takes that beak to blast his way out of that egg, kind of like the poet "leaving thine outgrown shell by life's unresting sea."

Oh that's what I want to do. I'm going to take in the bitter, the darkness, the rough places, the rain, the storms, the turmoil of life, take in all of my trials and tribulations until one day I'm going to blast my way out of this place to a land God promised me. A place where the wicked shall cease from troubling and the weary shall be at rest.

A DISCIPLE OF
LONG STANDING

———— ⧓ ————

Acts 21:16 (NKJV)

"Also some of the disciples from Caesarea
went with us and brought with them one,
Mnason of Cyprus, an early disciple ..."

I f I were to ask you what you know about the biblical character Paul, most of you could respond in some way. You would say that he was a Pharisee, that he took some missionary journeys, that he wrote some of the books of the New Testament, that he had a dramatic conversion experience on the Damascus Road. All of us know something about the Apostle Paul. The same goes for Simon Peter. Mention his name and we picture a rough fisherman called by Jesus to be a disciple. Peter was loud and aggressive. He always had something to say. He tried to walk on water once but started sinking into the water. He preached at Pentecost and three thousand were saved. His nickname was Rock. All of us know something about Simon Peter.

To a lesser degree, we could all come up with some information about James and John, and Andrew, and John the Baptist, and Zacchaeus. But what would you say if I asked about the New Testament character named Mnason? Most of you would say "Who?" Yet here in our text today is a man who one commentator says "is immortalized in eight words." Only eight words in the original Greek are written about this man. Yet what an intriguing picture is painted.

Mnason was a common Greek name. Among the Romans, the name was "Nason." "Jason" was the Jewish rendering of the name. Apparently, Mnason lived in Jerusalem. When Paul returned from his Gentile mission to Jerusalem, at a time when anything that threatened the idea of Jewish exclusiveness was looked on with suspicion, Mnason opened his home to Paul. His willingness to be Paul's host shows Mnason's gracious heart and hospitable spirit and also considerable courage in light of the situation. Notice the phrase used to describe Mnason in Acts 21:16. The King James Version calls him "an old disciple." The New Revised Standard Version refers to him as "an early disciple." The New English Bible says Mnason was "one who had been a believer since the early days." But in the New American Standard Bible, from which I have selected my title, from the Greek words, Mnsaon is described as "a disciple of long standing." Thinking on this phrase—a disciple of long standing—brought to my mind some sterling truths about the Christian life.

First, The Value Of Maturity

This phrase reminds us first of the value of maturity. The King James Version says Mnason was "an old disciple" The Greek word is translated best with the English word "Original." Mnason had been a disciple from the beginning. He had been a believer since the early days of the church. He was, as one translator suggests, "a foundation member of the church."

Why did Luke use that phrase to describe Mnason? Several commentators suggest that Luke's special mention of the fact that Mnason was one of the original Jerusalem disciples indicates that Luke acquired much valuable information about the earlier days of the church from him. Mnason had been around a long time. He had a broad base of experience from which to speak concerning the Christian faith. He was a mature believer.

How we need that kind of maturity in today's church. I am thankful for the blessed children of the church, for their freshness and openness is a constant challenge to the rest of us. I am thankful for the dynamic young people of the church, for their excitement and enthusiasm is contagious in its effect. I am thankful for the young adults in our churches, because their idealism and intensity motivate the rest of us. I am thankful for the middle-aged adults of our churches, because their dedication and determination provide the dynamism for our churches. Most of all, I am thankful for our older adult members, those who are "disciples of long standing," because they are the pillars who give stability to our churches.

Some say they are "over the hill." I say, if they are, then I hope they will tell us what it's like there so we can live our lives better as we approach the hill. Some say they are "has-beens." I say, if so, then I pray they will remind us of what has been so we can better prepare for what will be. Some say they are "just waiting to die." I say, if so, then I wish they would tell us what they have learned in their confrontation with the arithmetic of life so that we can make things add up better in our lives.

Some say all they can do anymore is pray. I say, if that is true, then pray for me and for our church and for the challenges before us. To those disciples of long standing in our churches today, I have this challenge: Don't retire from God's work. Don't withdraw from positions of responsibility. Don't hide your light under a bushel. Let it shine! For we need what you have to offer. There is nothing more valuable in the church than spiritual maturity.

Second, The Meaning Of Discipleship

A second truth evolves out of that phrase used to describe Mnason. Disciples of long standing are those who have discerned the true meaning of discipleship. Notice the two key facts about this man Mnason. He had been a disciple a long time, and he still was. The text not only calls attention to his long-term standing in the church. The key fact is that

Mnason was still active, still in good standing, still involved after all those years.

Mnason realized that discipleship is not just a one-time decision but a continuing process, not just a step but a walk. Discipleship does not end when a person walks down the aisle and professes faith in Christ. That's where discipleship begins. The greatest challenge facing many in today's church is to move past the decision for Christ and become a disciple of Christ.

A certain husband was surprised to find his wife at home when he came in from work. "I thought you were taking golf lessons," he said. She responded, "I didn't need any more golf lessons today. I learned how to play yesterday." Some people are like that about discipleship. When they obtained their discipleship at an earlier age, they set it in their spiritual trophy case. And they have been coasting ever since. The New Testament makes it very clear that a person does not drift into maturity in the Christian life. A person must discipline themselves into maturity. The Christian life is a race, and the bible admonishes us to "press on toward the mark." The Christian life is like a battle, and the bible urges us to "Put on the whole armor of God." The Christian life is like the physical development of a person from childhood to adulthood, and the bible challenges us to feed ourselves on the strong meat of God's word so that we can grow up spiritually. The Christian life is like building a house, and the bible exhorts us to build on the foundation of Jesus Christ a spiritual house that will bring honor to God. Every picture of the Christian life in the New Testament reminds us that it is a process that demands continued dedication and constant discipline on our part. Nobody drifts into maturity in the Christian life. Discipline is required. Maturity comes through faithful commitment to these five disciplines: **diligent study, regular worship, daily prayer, systematic giving, and personal witnessing.** When anyone—through dedication to these disciplines—becomes, like Mnason, a disciple of long standing, then that person has discovered the true meaning of discipleship.

Third and Finally, The Importance of Faithfulness

A third truth about the Christian life evolves from this phrase used to describe Mnason: the importance of faithfulness. Our text does not tell us much about Mnason. We do not know if he was a steward in the church. We do not know if he was a Sunday school teacher. We do not know if he ever served on a committee. We do not know if he could preach or sing. His name is immortalized in Holy Scriptures for one reason only: he was faithful to his lord. He never quit. He was faithful.

That is the one thing God expects of us. The only thing God demands of us is that we be faithful. Whether we have five talents or two talents or one talent, he wants us to do the best we can with what we have. He wants us to be faithful— nothing more and nothing less than that.

At a track meet, attention was focused on the mile run because one of the schools had a promising miler who had missed the state record in the mile by only one second the previous week. He was out to break the record in this meet. As the boys came to the starting mark, every eye was on him. He was tall, good-looking, a well-built kid. He looked like an athlete. As the eyes of the crowd swept the lineup of boys, they noticed at the other end of the line another boy who in every way was a sharp contrast to the gifted athlete I just mentioned. He was small of stature. His shoulders were narrow. He was hollow-chested. Even his legs were not straight. Everyone wondered what he was doing in the mile race.

When the race began, the favored athlete pushed off at a rapid pace. Every lap increased the distance between this star and the others. The little fellow fell behind. When the leader came around the final turn, the predicted winner sprinted the last one hundred yards. As he broke the tape, the crowd went into an uproar. He had established a new state record. Only a few others finished the race. Most of the runners dropped out when they saw they had no chance to win. As the field crews brought out the hurdles to set up for the next race, one of the judges shouted, "Get those hurdles out of the way! This Race is not over. Look! Around the turn came that hollow-chested, spindly-legged little boy, panting and staggering to keep going. Everybody in the audience stood silently and watched as he dragged the last hundred yards and literally fell across the finish line. One of the judges turned him over on his back and wiped the blood off his face with a handkerchief. The judge asked him, "Son, why didn't you drop out back there?" Between gasps for breath, the boy answered, "My school had a good miler, but he got sick a couple of days ago and couldn't run. The coach promised to have a man in every event, so he asked me if I'd come and run the mile." "Well, son," the man continued, "why didn't you just drop out? You were almost a lap behind." The boy answered, "Sir, they didn't send me here to win; they didn't send me here to quit. They sent me here to run this mile, and I ran it."

God didn't call us as Christians to win. He didn't' call us as Christians to quit. He commissioned us to run the race. If we run the race he has called us to run to the best of our ability, and refuse to give up, then someday each of us will be brought into the presence of the Heavenly Father and we will hear him say, "Well Done."

"If when you give the best of your service, telling the world that the savior is come, Be not dismayed, when men don't believe you, He'll understand and say, Well done.

"But if you try and fail in your trying, hands sore and scarred from the work you've begun, Take up your cross, run quickly to meet him, He'll understand and say, Well done."

CITIZENS OF TWO WORLDS

———— ⚬ ————

Ephesians 2: 19 (KJV)

*"Now therefore, ye are no more strangers
and foreigners, but fellow citizens with the
saints, and of the household of God."*

To be a citizen gives one a sense of nationalism, a sense of pride, and a sense of worthiness The idea that you belong to something and something belongs to you makes a person stand erect with self-respect. All men are citizens of one world. This world is the physical and material world. Man is a citizen of earth by habitation. He lives on earth, works and plays on earth. For clarification let us narrow the term "citizen of one world" to a citizen of the United States. All persons who are not citizens are aliens and foreigners. The alien does not have the opportunity to receive and enjoy the rights and privileges that are granted to citizens. The man or woman who is to live an abundant life of necessity must be a citizen of two worlds. The material world that he possesses by habitation, and the world of the spiritual, where man is measured by the good he does, and where intrinsic values are the means of exchange, and where ethics and morals govern the actions of men.

There are four ways that one may become a citizen of the United States. The first method is land tie—that is, to be born on American soil. The second is blood tie—that is, to be born of American parents. The third process is naturalization. And the fourth is legislation. This process is when people are made citizens by an act of Congress. The question arises: can an individual become a citizen of the kingdom of God by or through these methods? The answer is *no* to the procedures of the land tie, the process of naturalization, and legislation. However, the process of blood tie pertains to the kingdom Of God. The only way a person becomes a citizen of the kingdom of God, and a fellow citizen with the saints, is through the shed blood of Jesus Christ.

The man, woman, boy, or girl who is alien to God because of lust, transgression, and iniquity can, through due process of the cross, become a citizen of the realm of God. If he or she comes to God on his or her knees in prayer and supplication in the attitude of Charlotte Elliott, who wrote:

"Just as I am, without one plea, But that thy blood was shed for me, And that thou bidd'st me come to thee, O Lamb of God I come! I come! Just as I am and waiting not, to rid my soul of one dark blot, to thee, whose blood can cleanse each spot, O Lamb of God I come! I come!"

Yes, through the blood of Jesus we become fellow citizens with the saints. There are certain privileges that are granted citizens of our country. Persons who are not citizens are restrained and prohibited from participation in the acts of privilege. The citizen of the U.S. enjoys the privileges of participating in governmental affairs and electing governmental officials, and they are protected by the country in which they are a citizen.

The citizen of the kingdom of God has two special privileges, and they are: **the privilege of prayer and the privilege of the Holy Spirit** When trouble confronts us, when adversity prevails, when confusion is having the day, when the tempter draws nigh endeavoring to possess us, it is when we enjoy the privilege of prayer. To be able to talk with God, to commune with the Father of all humankind, is a most noble privilege. We live in a hostile universe in which neither science nor technology can give us power or hope. From this sense of powerlessness comes a need to appeal to something beyond us. We need to know that our lives are in touch with the power at the heart of the universe. Prayer is a way of making that contact. It is our way of reaching out for help. It is God's avenue of giving us help and strength.

Theodore Parker Ferris has said it for me: *"To be gentle in an age of violence; to be obedient in a time of reckless violation; to be honest in a day when extravagance and propaganda pay more than the truth; to love in a world full of hate; to hope in a world that is grim and dark; to hold fast to what is good in a world where it is hard to hold on to what you have ... you need all the help you can get."* As a citizen of the kingdom of God, you have that privilege.

The blessing of possessing the Holy Spirit is a most unique privilege. When we attune our hearts and minds to the melody of heaven, when all vain and idle thoughts depart from our minds, when our hearts are freed from hatred, prejudice, and malice. Like the Apostles of old we become of one accord. The spirit of God descends upon us. Our souls rejoice and our hearts are happy.

One day I went out to start my car and discovered it wouldn't start. I started pushing buttons and turning knobs trying to blow the horn to determine what the problem was. So I called AAA and waited for them to arrive. He pulled into my yard—he pulled alongside of my car. He got out the jumper cables, hooked the two batteries together, started the truck, and I turned the key to mine. The surge of energy from the good battery was all it took.

Do you know why the possessing of the Holy Spirit is a privilege? Because the Holy Spirit performs a similar function in the lives of believers. He comes alongside to assist us. His power strengthens our weaknesses, his guidance makes up for our short-sightedness; his compassion warms the coldness of our hearts. He continues to recharge our batteries when we attune our hearts and minds to the melody of heaven. The citizens of the realm of God pleads for the privilege of enjoying God's spirit. That is why we pray: "Come Holy Spirit, Heavenly Dove, With all thy quickening power; Kindle a flame of sacred love in these cold hearts of ours. Look how we grovel here below, Fond of these earthly toys; Our souls how heavily they go, to reach eternal joys!"

With all privileges there are an equal amount of responsibilities. Many would accept the privileges granted by citizenship. Yes, there are multitudes who seek out the privileges offered. But there are but a few individuals who seek out the responsibilities.

As a citizen of the United States we have the responsibility to maintain the federal government by the paying of taxes. We also have the responsibility of defending the shores, possessions, and ideals of the United States by taking up of arms. Yes, he who accepts the privileges of this country must march to the cadence of the stars and stripes to defend the homeland.

Likewise there are grave responsibilities in regard to the kingdom of God. The citizens of the realm of God have to fight to protect the standards of the Christ within and without. The citizen must find the strength to withstand all of the jibes and prejudices, all of the subtle hatreds, and discriminations with the rare courtesy that is the armor of pure souls. Christians must not be afraid to fight against the law, the grasping, the wicked, the unbending righteousness that is the sword of the just. We are soldiers in God's army! Sometimes the battle gets hot and we are wounded and even killed in the battle to protect the standards of Christ. But we, as responsible Christians, must not release our grip on our faith in Jesus Christ.

There is a story of a young soldier who was ordered to plant the U.S. flag on a hilltop that was being contested by the enemy. In the line of duty, the flag was blown to bits and the young man was killed in battle. When the battle was over and the victory won, the captain observed that although this young soldier had been killed in the battle, he never released his grip on the flagstaff. In our daily battle against temptation, against paying evil for evil, of not being neighborly, we must not let go of the staff. It's our responsibility to hold up the blood-stained banner even if it's nothing but the staff.

"If when you give the best of your service, telling the world that the savior is come; be not dismayed when men don't believe you; he understands; he'll say well done."

Many today would accept the privilege of prayer and of the Holy Spirit, but they prefer not to accept the responsibilities of Christianity. The question is asked, "What is the chief responsibility of a Christian?" Let the master himself answer that question: "Thou shalt love the lord thy God with all thy heart, with all thy mind, and with all thy strength ... and love thy neighbor as thyself."

Yes, we who would be fellow citizens with saints must heed the answer of Jesus and accept our responsibility with the glory of our privileges. Soon and very soon the battle will be over. One morning as we shall sit gazing out upon the sea of time, we will feel the hinges of the gate of life getting rusty, and as the evening steals on and the night star rises, a wind will blow out of the west, and blow our physical gate ajar, and our soul will fly like an eagle across the sea of time.

> **"In the morning, the dewdrops of happiness will greet the dawn.**
>
> **In the morning, the dove of peace will be cooing in the halls of justice.**

In the morning, I shall bid farewell to this land of sorrow and I shall join the church triumphant I shall join the church where fellow citizens with the saints and present my claim to that mansion prepared for me"

DO WE LOOK
FOR ANOTHER?

———— $\propto$ ————

Matthew 11:3 (NKJV)

*"And said to him, Are you the coming
one, or do we look for another?"*

T his question was first asked by John, who was sent
by God to set the stage for the appearance of Jesus
Christ. John the Baptizer appeared almost out of
nowhere and began preaching and attracting the attention
of the Jews in Jerusalem and Judea. People went to hear
him preach, and amazingly, they responded to his message
by coming forward—entering the river—to be baptized by
this ascetic-looking religious phenomenon. He prepared
the way of the Lord by preaching and baptizing in the River
Jordan. When Jesus appeared on the banks of the Jordan,
John introduced him as "the Lamb of God that taketh away
the sins of the world." He says, "After me comes one who is
mightier than I, the thong of whose sandals I am not worthy
to stoop down and untie. I have baptized you with water, but

he will baptize you with the Holy Spirit." He presented Jesus as the completion and the crown of humanity's salvation. Beyond Christ there could not be another. Yet John was not totally satisfied with the fact that Jesus Christ was the greatest expression and the profoundest proof for the existence of God. Could it be that while John was in prison awaiting his death, he needed to know for sure if Jesus was the one, or should they look for another? John's doubt is our doubt. Every now and then we ask ourselves, "Are you the coming one, or do we look for another?" Jesus did not come up to his personal expectation for John. At first John was sure without a doubt that Christ was he who should come or had come. But now, sitting in the prison fortress of Machaerus, he was unsettled, unsure, and unstable.

In this modern-day technological and scientific discovery we have lost our spiritual balance. I don't believe we are as sure about Christ as we ought to be today. We are reeling and rolling from side to side like a drunken man looking for Christ or another. I think this is what happened in the Jonestown incident a few years ago. Those people who died lost their spiritual balance. They were not sure of the Christ so they looked for another and found death by poison. We'd better hurry up and answer that question today before we ourselves become victims of circumstances. If you have not answered the question, then you can be sure that a whole lot of Jim Joneses will answer it for you. We need to settle that question today. So this question before should be answered by you today and be sure within ourselves that he is the Christ we need for this world today. If Christ is not the one…

It Raises Doubts as to The Finality of Christ as Savior of The World

John says, "He is the Lamb of God that taketh away the sins of the world.... Prepare ye the way of the Lord, Make his paths straight." Is he actually the Lamb of God or is he still to come. Do we look for another? There has been an increase of movements today that cause Christians who are unstable in their faith to raise doubts as to who Christ is. There is fear, which comes because many young people are joining cults and other mind-boggling groups. So the question of "Are you the one or look we for another?" is being asked in many homes, schools, groups, and the like. In the seminary I had a course in the history of religions. The instructor voiced an appreciation for the worth and beauty of many religions. He said that Christianity picked up most of its contents from older religions. He concluded that Christianity was the sort of faith that will finally be absorbed in a sort of synthesis with Mohammedism, Buddhism, Hinduism, or Confucianism. In short the author left one with the uncertainty as to whether Jesus is the Savior of the World or Mohammed.

Christianity is a very young religion. The resurrection had been here in operation before Christianity was born. Williston Walker states, "Christianity entered no empty world. Its Advent found men's minds filled with conceptions of the universe, of religion, of sin, of rewards and punishments with which it had to reckon with and adjust itself." Even though Christianity is young, it is important because as a late phenomenon it has transcended all other religions. The other major religions have risen, flourished, reached their apex, and then have entered a slow decline or have become stationary. Hinduism is not as widely practiced as it was fifteen hundred years ago. Buddhism had considerable losses for a period of time. Confucianism has achieved no great geographic advance since it moved into Korea and Japan. Christianity is still only in the first flush of its history and it is still growing in the life of humankind.

Even today, with the rise of Unitarian groups operating under the guise of Christian churches, Christianity will not disappear nor will it fully triumph within history. These Unitarian groups are teaching young minds that Christ is not divine, that he is not God's final, ultimate answer for man's redemption, that Christ did not die for the sins of the world, that he is not God. They firmly hold that we are not bound by Christ's command to repent, to believe and be baptized. This kind of heresy denounces the doctrine of heaven and hell and leaves us to ask the question, "Are you the coming one, or do we look for another?"

This is the kind of instability that leads many people away from Christ into the doctrines of false prophets. We must be sure that Christ is the final, unconditional answer for us. Christ just doesn't want us to know him but demands our unconditional surrender. Christ is All in All!

Second, It Raises Doubts As To Whether Christ Completely Satisfies.

John was confronted by several religious sects. There were the Saduccees, who were of the Aristocratic society influenced by worldly rulers; the Pharisees, who believed strictly in the laws as being handed down from Moses to be observed; the Essenes, who were the ascetics who did not drink and told others of their shortcomings and were deeply hated by the people; the Zealots, who advocated freedom from the foreign control and that God wanted them to be free. All of these had different views about life and human destiny. Into that religious syncretism, Jesus came, saying, "I am the Way, the Truth, and the Life, no man comes to the Father, but by me." He came saying, "Come unto me all ye that labor and are heavy laden, and I will give you rest." He came saying, "These things have I spoken unto you, that your joy might remain in you, and that your joy might be full." No other religion can satisfy as the Christian religion.

Even when Christ was about to make his departure from this world, Philip said unto him, "Lord, show us the Father and it is sufficient for us." Jesus turned and said unto him, "Have I been so long time with you, and yet you have not known me, Philip? He who has seen me has seen the Father." There is no satisfaction beyond the experience of seeing the Father. People today are searching for a Christ that satisfies. When they don't find him, they look for another.

A story is told of a Christian woman trying to be persuaded by one of Father Divine's followers. She told the persuader, "I had better check Father Divine out. I heard he was born in Georgia. The reply was Yes! Well, let me tell you something; "My Christ is from everlasting to everlasting". People in search of personal satisfaction want to find a Christ; one who walks beside you, one who sticks closer than a brother. The old religions before Christianity could not satisfy. Even Judaism could not satisfy. Paul was a strict

Judaistic religionist but he was not really satisfied until he met Christ on the Damascus Road. What happened to Saul (Paul) can happen to many today. ", No other name, no other faith satisfies than the Christ-Jesus of Nazareth when you know that Christ satisfies, you can be in a prison cell and find satisfaction. You can travel to the ends of the earth, but no other name can satisfy the inner discontentment of your soul. When you know Christ nothing else matters. **Finally, The Question Must Be Answered.**

It must be answered because one is sure it will erase the doubts that arise from an unchecked faith. There is no faith as expressive as the Christian faith. The eleventh chapter of Hebrews has been called the Magna Carta of Faith that tells the story of the faithful **"who through faith subdued kingdoms, worked righteousness obtained promises, stopped the mouths of lions, quenched the violence of fire, escaped the edge of the sword, out of weakness were made strong, became valiant in battle, turned to fight the armies of the aliens; they were stoned, they were sawn in two, were tempted, were slain with the sword, they wandered about in sheepskins and goat-skins, being destitute, afflicted, tormented; of whom the world was not worthy. These all died in faith, not having received the promise but having seen them afar off"**

There is no use looking for another. Something happens to an individual in Christ that nothing seems to take away the inner joy that they have. When Polycarp, at the age of eighty-six, met his death under Marcus Aurelius during the Fourth Persecution, he was condemned to be burned alive.

He prayed while he was bound to the stake. Fire was set to the body on both sides. He began to sing praises to God in the midst of the flames and he was not consumed. When the guards stuck spears into his body, the blood put the fire out. He cried, "Eighty-six years have I served him; he has never failed me."

No other religion is as expressive as the religion of Jesus Christ my Lord! Nobody could make him shut up about his saving faith in Jesus Christ. It's a known fact that no other religion has inspired people to run, scream, shout, and rejoice like the Christian religion. And these overt expressions are from people who have found Christ to be their all in all.

It inspired Fannie Crosby to write, "Pass me not O Gentle Savior, Hear my humble cry, While on others thou are calling, DO NOT PASS ME BY. ... I'm calling SAVIOR! SAVIOR!!"

It inspired the two disciples to go back to tell John after meeting Jesus that "The blind receive their sight; the lame can walk; the lepers are cleansed; the deaf hear; the dead are raised up and the poor have the gospel preached to them." There is no need to look for another! He is the Christ, the Son of God, He is Mary's baby, He is the lamb of God, He is the Rock of Ages, He is the Lily of the Valley, the Bright and Morning Star!

SOMETHING TO HOLD ON TO

---— ⋈ ——---

II Timothy 1:12 (NKJV)

"For I know whom I have believed and am persuaded that he is able to keep what I have committed to him until that day.

A poem was written years ago by William Butler Yeats titled "The Second Coming." In that poem are these immortal words: "Things fall apart; the center cannot hold." This poem was considered a lyric that held a century together. It was written out of difficulty when Britain and Europe were reeling from the devastation of World War I, the Russian Revolution, and the Easter Rebellion, which had already rocked Ireland. Perhaps this is why the poem is pessimistic. The events of recent history had shattered the idealism of the late nineteenth century. It is no wonder that the poet Yeats

wrote: "The blood-dimmed tide is loosed, and everywhere the ceremony of innocence is drowned."

No wonder he felt that "things fall apart; the center cannot hold." We celebrated the birthday of Dr. Martin Luther King Jr., and as I sat in the convention center wondering what Dr. King would have to say to us today as things fall apart—crime, racism, gun violence, the moral fabric of our nation is falling apart.

In his book *Strength to Love*, Dr. King writes, "At the center of the Christian Faith is the conviction that in the universe there is a God of power who is able to do exceedingly abundant things in nature and in history. The God we serve is not a weak and incompetent God." I believe he would have that to say to us in 2019, as things in our lives fall apart. It is faith in him that we must rediscover. He is able to give us the power, the inner equilibrium to stand tall amid the trials and burdens of life. "Things fall apart; the center cannot hold." God is able to give us something to hold on to if we put our trust in him.

What a contrast Yeats's poem is to Timothy's letter from the Apostle Paul. There are similarities. Like Yeats, Paul was facing difficult times. He is writing from prison in Rome, and everyone deserted him except for Luke, the faithful physician. It is a dark and dismal time. He tells Timothy, "I am already being poured out like a drink offering, and the time of my departure has come. I have fought a good fight, I have finished the race, I have kept the faith." There would be good reason for this to be a depressing letter, but instead it reverberates with this bold affirmation: "I know whom I have believed, and am persuaded that he is able to keep what I have committed to him until that day." The apostle had found something to hold on to, a central affirmation for his life, which filled him with confidence even in the hour of death.

I pulled back from the letter and asked the question I suspect Timothy asked: "Paul, where did you find that center?" How can I develop the kind of faith that can be a solid center for my own soul? Where can I find that kind of confidence for hard and difficult times? I found Paul's answer in verse 13: "Hold fast the pattern of sound words which you have heard from me, in faith and love which are in Christ Jesus." In the third chapter, Paul expands on this confidence to Timothy: "And that from childhood you have known the Holy Scriptures, which are able to make you wise for salvation through faith which is in Christ Jesus. All Scripture is given by inspiration of God, and is profitable for doctrine, for reproof, for correction, for instruction in righteousness. That the man of God may be complete, thoroughly equipped for every good work" (II Tim 3:15–17).

If we are to find something to hold on to, if we are to stand up and say "I believe," if we are to be fully equipped for the good life God intends for us, then we must become, in the words of John Wesley, people of "One Book": men and women whose live are nourished by scripture, shaped by the written witness to the living word of God.

Let me give you an example of this truth. In 1981 his name had not become a global household word; he had not yet received the Nobel Peace Prize. Desmond Tutu was just a bishop in South Africa, serving as the executive secretary of the South African Council of Churches. He was called before a commission of inquiry set up to investigate the council. Picture clearly in your mind a small black man confronting all the awesome fury of apartheid. And what did he talk about? He talked about the Bible. He said: "You whites brought us the bible, now we blacks are taking it seriously. We are involved with God to set us free from all that enslaves us and makes us less than what he intended us to be. The Bible is the most revolutionary, the most radical book there is. If any book should be banned by those who rule unjustly and as tyrants, it is the bible."

Bishop Tutu led his judges through a profound study of how the God of history liberates the oppressed and concluded with this courageous affirmation that we are now beginning to see fulfilled: "I want the government to know now and always that I do not fear them. They are trying to defend the utterly indefensible and they will fail. They will fail because they are ranging themselves on the side of evil and injustice against the church of God."

Here's how a secular newspaper described the scene: "The Commissioners stared stonily ahead of them. ... Tutu leaned back, closed the old leather-bound Bible he had been brandishing and mopped his brow. A rearguard battle in the theological civil war had been fought and won."

Any creed that dares to call itself an expression of the Christian faith must be grounded in scripture. If we are to have the kind of faith that will equip us for every kind of good deed, if we are to find something to hold on to in difficult times, if we are to know whom we have believed, then we must read, study, discuss, devour, and nourish our souls on the witness of the written word. "Hold Firmly," Paul said, "to the true words that I taught you."

Paul also tells Timothy to "be strong in the grace that is in Christ Jesus." That sounds like friendship. You cannot read this letter without feeling the passion and intensity in Paul's friendship with Timothy. The letter overflows with it. Paul writes: "I remember you constantly in my prayers night and day. Recalling your tears, I long to see you that I may be filled with joy. Do your best to come to me soon" (II Tim 1:3–4; 4:9).

When was the last time you wrote a letter like that? How long as it been since you remembered the face of a friend who was so much a part of your life, so deeply bound up with your soul that you could not help thinking of them night and day? How long has it been since you shared someone's tears? When was the last time you wrapped your arms around a brother or sister in the love of Christ? If you want to find something to hold on to, then practice the gift of Christian friendship.

We are the church, the "Koinonia"—the fellowship of kindred mind. What we believe when we repeat our creeds, the community is called together to meet one another at their need. The community of faith came first, and the creeds grew out of their life together as the declaration of a new identity in Christ Jesus. For Christian people, there is no belief that is not a shared belief, no theology that is not born out of community, no creed that is not strengthened in friendship. As John Wesley reminded us, "There is no holiness that is not social holiness."

In my years in ministry, I've seen people face tough times. I have become convinced as I have observed people in difficult times that there really are just two kinds of people in this world: those who discover the power of friendship and those who don't. There are those who open their lives to someone else, who allow a friend to invade the inner sanctum of their souls, who share themselves in the love of Christ. And when the tough times come, these persons find nourishment, courage, strength, and hope in their relationships. Then there are persons who are independent, self-sufficient, to stand alone. And when tough times come, that's exactly where they are: independent and alone. We are part of this community of the crucified one. Barriers of race and class and sex have no place in the community. We are defined and identified by the company we keep—the community in which we claim our identity.

Be strong through the grace that is ours in union with Christ Jesus. This sounds like what Jesus said to his disciples on the night before he died: "Greater love has no one than this, than to lay down one's life for his friends. No longer do I call you servants, for a servant does not know what his master is doing, but I have called you friends, for all things that I heard from my father I have made known to you" (John 15:13–15).

Paul also reminds Timothy "of the help of the Holy Spirit living in us." Paul thinks back to the day he laid his hands on Timothy's head and confirmed him in the faith—the way we lay hands on the heads of those persons whom we are setting aside for special service in the ministry. "I remind you to rekindle the gift of God that is within you through the laying on of my hands, for God did not give us a spirit of timidity, or fear, but rather a spirit of power and of love and of self discipline."

In the early days of my youth, we used records, like a forty-five with a big hole in the middle of the record. You would need a big spindle to fill it. There is a big hole in the center of our souls that can only be filled with the living, loving, life-giving spirit of God. We try to fill it with all sorts of other things—success, power, prestige, money, sex, influence— but it is like a huge, internal sinkhole that will swallow up all the puny things we try to stuff into it, and it will leave us empty and dry. There was an article that appeared in *Jet* magazine that there were some forty African-Americans out of the 120 members in the Branch Davidian cult. I was shocked to learn that there were so many black people in the cult. Dr. Alvin Poussaint was asked the question, "What kind of person would follow someone like David Koresh?" His response was:

Someone who is very religious, or religious-oriented, and also very lonely. I think somewhat dependent and are looking for a family, a group to which they can really feel they belong and they're somebody. They're prone to follow charismatic authority without question, they become true believers and show an absence of independent thought. It becomes blind faith, which makes it difficult for you to reach them. These are people searching for something to hold on to.

We can become that model, that support person, that church sitting on a hill that cannot be hidden. We must let our lights so shine for them to see we are what you need.

It is through the church that we must develop strong family relationships and help develop proper values and boost self-confidence in children so they won't grow up and be attracted to cults or gangs. There is only one thing in this universe that is big enough to fill the empty space in our souls; it is the Spirit of God. Pentecost has already happened. The gift has already been given. The spirit is alive and present within and among God's people. God's spirit is the spirit of love, power, and a sound mind. When we nourish the presence of the spirit in our lives, then regardless of whatever happens, we are never alone.

H. G. Spafford was a businessman who lost everything in the great Chicago fire. While he was trying to rebuild his business, he sent his wife and four daughters on a voyage to Great Britain to visit relatives, planning to take a later voyage and meet them there. On November 22, 1873, there was an accident at sea. The liner was rammed by another ship and sank immediately. Mrs. Spafford was saved, but all four daughters were lost. When she arrived in England, she sent a two-word telegram to her husband: "Saved alone."

Spafford took the next ship to meet her. When his ship reached the place where the ship his family traveled on had gone down, the captain notified the passengers of the location. Spafford said he spent a sleepless night, tumbling and turning in sorrow. Finally, he wrote his feelings down, and they came out in poetry and later were put into a song:

When Peace like a river, attendeth my way, when sorrows like sea billows roll,

Whatever my lot, thou hast taught me to say,

It is well, it is well with my Soul

Works cited

King, Martin Luther Jr. *Strength to Love*. James Washington.Harper San Francisco. 1991

Spafford, H. G. "It Is Well with My Soul." (A.M.E. Zion Bicentennial Hymnal #507) October 1996 Charlotte, NC

MAKING THE MOST OF ONESELF

———— ✂ ————

I Corinthians 3:10 (NIV)

"By the grace God has given me, I laid a foundation as an expert builder, and someone else is building on it. But each one should be careful how he builds."

What shall I make of myself? This is one of life's greatest questions. Every successful individual who has satisfactorily answered the question has made a definite contribution to the social order. Our chief duty is to make the best and the most of ourselves.

The Apostle Paul's metaphor likening the development of the church to a building project is a good metaphor for self-actualization, for building a tower of a life. And make no mistake about it: life is a building project that demands purposefulness, creativity, and courage. E. E. Cummings is reported to have said, "It takes courage to grow up and be who you really are." Among the imperatives in making the most of one's self that are shown through the speaker of our text, we find (1) the ability to choose wisely, (2) the powerful influence of an ideal, and (3) symmetrical development of our lives. They are established as the most important factors in a well-balanced life.

First, consider the ability to choose wisely. Paul speaks of builders choosing to care how they build. Lying at the very root of personal development is the perilous power of choice. Within each of us is a self-determining power, which is the engine of the will. Within us lies that mental lever that we can choose to pull to determine our course in life and the quality of that course. Thomas Carlyle said: "For the same material one builds palaces, another builds hovels, one warehouses, one builds villas. Bricks and mortar are mortar and bricks until the architect makes them into something else. Thus, it is that, in the same family, in the same circumstances, one builds, a stately mansion, while his brother, vacillating and incompetent, lives forever amid ruins."

Each of us must make a life-determining choice. Not choosing is itself a choice. We cannot go far on the journey of life before we reach the point where we must choose the course we will take. Success and failure are often determined in the beginning of the race of life. Therefore, we should choose wisely, for as John Oxenham said: To every man there openeth. A way, and ways, and a way.

The high soul climbs the high way, the low soul gropes the low;

And in between, on the misty flats, the rest drift to and fro.

But to every man there openeth a High way and a Low way,

And each man decideth the way his soul shall go.

However, without the company of noble ideals from which to choose, choice is an abandoned child. Paul's noble ideal is personified in the life and teachings of Jesus, the "foundation." When we have a task we want to accomplish, a condition we want to attain, or any purpose at all, we form a mind-concept of the thing desired. This is called an ideal. We must have an ideal if we are to become what we are capable of becoming. The artist first conceives in her mind the work she sets forth to accomplish. First the ideal, then the canvas, the clay, or the granite and long hours of toil, and finally the finished product.

When the architect builds a house, the plans are drawn that the workers follow. The idea is the soul's plan upon the drawing board. Where there is no ideal, there is no development, no progress, no attainment; rather just as the worker without a detailed plan could not build a house but only a heap of stones, the person without an ideal drifts and usually degenerates.

When the orchestra plays, it follows the score of the composer. The ideal is the soul's score. Without it the soul is disordered, torn, and unhappy—just as there would be only wild discord if all the musicians in the orchestra played as they pleased without considering one another.

When a ship leaves port, the captain knows where he or she wants to go. To the soul, the ideal is the same as the captain's destination. Most people who never "arrive" fail because they have no goal. They sail aimlessly. They mistake motion for progress, and often that motion is in a circle. Ever moving yet never arriving.

Get an ideal! "Hitch your wagon to a star" and move on. Make every deed, every dream bend toward your objective. To make the most of your life and opportunities, have an ideal of the kind of life you want to live—the kind of person you desire to be, the position you wish to occupy, the career you desire—and move on. Move on through the darkness because you believe in the coming of the morning.

> Move on and do, knowing that we live in
> deeds, not years; in thoughts, not breaths.
>
> Move on—through floods and flames
> because victory is beyond.
>
> Move on—through your Gethsemanes,
> up your Calvarys.
>
> Move on—from weakness to strength,
> from defeat to victory until the ideal leads
> you into the fullness of Christlike living.

Finally, in our efforts to make the most of ourselves, we must strive for the symmetrical development of our lives—development in the moral realm, where character is formed. There we have an almost limitless range in which to make the most of ourselves. Our lives must have length, breadth, and height. By length, I do not refer to life's duration in time but rather to its forward push in self-development. By breadth, I mean life's outreach; by height, I mean its up-reach toward God.

Our ambition may place before us a shining mark toward which we strive with all possible energy and haste. But in our mad rush toward the distant goal, we may lose sight of and interest in all other things about us. A life developed in this way may show great energy, but it is essentially narrow and selfish—a life with length but without breadth or height. Another life develops laterally. It is full of tender sympathies, sending out a thin cloud over everything and everyone, but it descends in refreshing rain nowhere. Far-reaching but nebulous, it lacks concentration. This life has breadth without length or height.

Then there is the life that ignores the world and all worldly things. It shuts itself in, leaving only a small opening toward the heavens. Faith without flesh and piety without passion, this life has height without length or breadth. What is needed to balance all these extremes is a combination of the qualities that give life length, breadth, and height—forward push, outreach, and up-reach. In order to make the most of oneself, one must be motivated by far-reaching drive, a widespread love, and an uplifting faith.

Then there is the pivotal role of divine grace that the Apostle Paul well understood. Paul insists that if he made any contribution at all, if he built anything at all, if he laid any kind of foundation at all, it was according to the grace of God: "by the Grace God has given me." In the end, see it is not our choices or our ideas or even perfect symmetry in development that has the most influence on our making a life; rather it is all these things anointed by God's grace. God's grace, the nurturing water of God's sustaining love, feeds and grows us. Thus, we wisely choose and idealize always in the nurturing presence of God, laying hold of an active energy, an undaunted courage, and unfailing purpose through a vital faith in God. We should ask as an unknown writer did:

Help me to choose, O Lord, from out of the maze
And multitudes of things that by me roll,
One thing to work on and pray for here on earth-
Something to keep before me as a goal;
That when I die my days may form for thee,
Not many fragments but one perfect whole.
I seek, O Lord, some purpose in my life,
Some end which will my daily acts control,
So my days seem wasted now to me-
All disconnected hours that by me roll,
Help me to choose, O Lord, while I am young,
Something to keep before as a goal.

Works cited

Anonymous. "Help Me to Choose."

Oxenham, John. "The Ways" in *Best Loved Poems of the American People*, ed. Hazel Felleman (New York: Doubleday, 1936).

You Can Go Anywhere from Nowhere

———— ∝ ————

Luke 2:1–7

S ince this isn't Christmas, and we're not bound by seasonal traditions, let me invite you to go with me to Bethlehem, this time with a whole new set of rules. There won't be any carols and definitely not any songs about "poor little Jesus Child." I will not deal with the desk clerk at the inn nor will I dwell on the shepherds. This is a sermon on how people born in poverty can rise to unexpected places. I can think of such persons like the Late Rev. Dr. Leon Sullivan, the founder of Opportunities Industrialization Centers (OIC), International foundation for Education and Self-Help, and Progress Non- Profit Charitable Trust. *The Sullivan Principles*, which he authored, were instrumental in bringing an end to apartheid in South Africa. His book *Moving Mountains* tells how this son born in Appalachian poverty can use his mind to bring about change in the human heart. He never forgot where he came from. He made it his business to see that no one would be left behind. This is an inspiring story of one who believed that you can go any-where from nowhere.

The Sullivan Principles, says Rev. Jesse Jackson, should be required reading for every American child as the Pledge of Allegiance and the Bill of Rights are. Another person I read about is the Autobiography of Reverend Doctor Robert Schuller, of the Crystal Cathedral. His autobiography is My Journey: From an Iowa Farm to a Cathedral of Dreams. He says, "I was born at the dead end of a dirt road that had no name and no number." He believed that one could rise from humble beginnings to be whatever you set your heart and mind to. His possibility thinking on self esteem led millions to believe that you can go anywhere from nowhere. And so in the text that I selected I want us to take this trip to Bethlehem but not for the same reasons we go every year. On this trip to Bethlehem we find no reason to pity Jesus. He has two loving parents who love him dearly but at times find him awfully different. He has the usual ten fingers and ten toes, and the normal feelings and mental equipment. There really is no reason to pity Jesus, because so many of us (like Sullivan, Schuller) started at the socioeconomic bottom. Given what Jesus had, so far as raising children is concerned, it could even be a parental advantage to start at the same kind of lowest point on the totem pole of human society.

Maybe God is trying to show us that there's nothing wrong starting at the bottom in society. There are some advantages in starting from the bottom. God wanted to identify with the oppressed through a human son. Existential philosophers would easily explain this on the basis that people at the bottom always see a society more accurately than others. They have no vested interests to maintain, and no positions of privilege to protect. Jesus's matchless clarity of insight about people and society was at least partially due to his being a "manger kid," accurately sizing his world up, as first seen from the very bottom.

Jesus's start at the bottom even fits best with God's goal of the salvation of the world. If Jesus had been king, he would not have been accessible to the masses. Even a middle-class merchant's family would still have left him out of the reach of many. But all may feel close to him, regardless of the condition of their birth, because Jesus started at a level where all could feel free to approach him, with no fear of being put down.

In reading the Gospel of Matthew, one wonders if he really understood since he often overlooked data for the belief that God specifically meant for Jesus to be identified with at the bottom. Look at the first chapter of Matthew and read the genealogy and see how Matthew breaks with tradition and mentions four women in the first six verses. Mind you, these women were not respectable by some societies' standards. Take Rahab; she was at one time an outright prostitute. Then there were people like Ruth and Tamar, and Bathsheba, the unprotesting widow of the murdered Uriah. All of these women have what might be called character flaws, and they are in Jesus's family. In fact, almost everyone in Jesus's family tree had flaws. Matthew is telling us of a racial mixture and strange arrangements in the ancestry of a Savior whose background was as mixed and as questionable as ours. But I believe that God had that in the plan all along. Jesus carried his identification with the folks at the bottom even further. In the parable of the last judgment, Jesus said the unforgettable words, "Inasmuch as ye did it unto the least of my loved ones, ye did it unto me."

This also suggests that God, who is all-wise and -knowing, who is no respecter of persons, will provide leadership for us from the least likely places. It doesn't matter where you started; just try to figure out where God wants you to end up.

I suppose the most important reason for this revisitation of Bethlehem and the stable is to help us celebrate our own mangers and stables—our own obscure and unimpressive beginnings. You see, if we can be glad about our own starting places, we need never be ashamed before anybody. If we can rejoice over our own little tiny birthplaces, we can be glad God made us there, and we can be willing to go back if ever the need should arise. We can be free of the fear that we might have to go back to where we started.

But we can be like the rabbit in the old tale told by ancestors. When the powerful, vicious fox was about to eat up the rabbit and have him for lunch, the rabbit pleaded, "Oh please, Mr. Fox, do anything to me but please don't eat me." This appealed to the cruel instincts of the fox. He could just see the rabbit suffering from the thorns of the briar patch. The fox could imagine Mr. Rabbit's terrible misery, so he threw him into the thicket. It was a great victory for Br'er Rabbit, because he was born and reared in briars. He knew how to deal with briars, and he laughed at the fox as he ran and leaped to safety. There are so manger kids from the ghetto, and the lower social status of society, living on one meal a day, and poor housing conditions. We can thank God for our mangers, because we can survive anytime, anywhere, and under any circumstances. This text tells us one's outlook is never blind to Promised Land challenges. Martin Luther King said on the eve of his death that "we as a people will get to the Promised Land." But I want to remind you that there is no such thing as a Promised Land ready-made for occupancy. There are giants in the land. One's outlook should never be blind to the opposition, obstacles, and oppression that must be overcome. Behind every successful and admirable person is a story of struggle, pain, and sacrifice.

I. You Cannot Move Into Your Future In The Promised Land If You Are Hung Up On Your Past In Egypt.

You cannot move forward with backward thinking. You cannot walk backward into the future. The children of Israel kept rebelling against their future by telling Moses that they wanted to go back to what God had delivered them from. Looking and thinking backward are always dangerous when God is calling us forward. Lot's wife looked back to Sodom and became a pillar of salt. Jesus warned, "No one having put his hand to the plow, and looking back is fit for the kingdom of God."

As long as you are looking and thinking backward, what is behind you will define and confine you. The pain in our past is always pulling at us and trying to make prisoners out of us. Do you remember the times when hotels used a key to get into rooms? Then all of a sudden they switched to cards that you slide in, like credit cards. Try using a key to get into a hotel room and see how far you get. There are some old keys that will preclude us from getting into the room of new opportunities in the new millennium. Old habits, attitudes, and biases will not open the door to the new era. We must live in the power of the future and never let where we come from or where we started keep us from getting what God has for us. With God where you are going can overrule the influence of where you have been and what you have painfully experienced. Some of you are afraid of the future because matters of the past keep coming at you, but God has opened up the way so that you can move to the divinely designed place.

II. This Text Says With God In Us, With Us, We Can Conquer The Challenges Before Us.

The reason why you often can look back down the same path and see the past and future is that a glance at what was should motivate us to move forward into what can be. When you look over your shoulder and see what you have been through, that gives you a reason to move ahead. When you look back and see the negative and nasty things that you have had to deal with yesterday, that glimpse should make you run into tomorrow. You hurry because you do not want to relive that pain; you do not want to relive that tragedy. So when you see your past behind you, then you ought to move with determination into the place that God has set before you.

If you set your eyes on God, nothing can keep you from your destiny. Joshua and Caleb told the people to have faith in God, that if God was for them, no one could defeat them. That's the same message for you too. Faith will empower you to step up and become who you are divinely designed to be. Faith enables you to step up. How do we step up? In Number 14:9 it says, "Only do not rebel against the Lord, nor fear the people of the land, for they are our bread; their protection has departed from them, and the Lord is with us." What Joshua and Caleb were saying was, "But the Lord." Those are three words that can change any condition. "But the Lord" will encourage the discouraged, free the frustrated, and heal the hurting. Three words: "But the Lord." Is your money running funny and your change strange? Remember "But the Lord." There is a child strung out on drugs and you think they are not coming back, Remember, "but the Lord." Though a host should encamp against me, "but the Lord." You can go any-where from nowhere because of "But the Lord."

III. You Can Go Anywhere And Claim The Promise When You Know Who You Are.

Jesus willingly stepped down, says Apostle Paul in Philippians when he says "Let this mind be in you, which was also in Christ Jesus: who, being in the form of God, did not consider equality with God, a status to be clung to." Jesus joined the people at the bottom and assumed the role of a lowly servant, and was made in the likeness of a human being. "And being in human form, he humbled himself and became obedient to death itself, even the death of the cross." Jesus knew who he was and took the embarrassment out of Bethlehem beginnings and manger cradles. Joshua and Caleb claimed what God had promised because they knew who they were and where the Lord was taking them. When you know who you are, you can make and seize opportunity because your spirituality informs, emancipates, and empowers your mentality, which enables you to grasp greatness and possess what God has promised. When you know who you are your "in look" shapes your outlook, and your outlook creates your outcome. When it comes to how you view you, what you see is what you get.

A story is told of a young man who everyone referred to as Mercedes. That was not his real name, and he did not drive a Mercedes. As a college student, he drove a used Pinto, a used Nova, and a used Pacer that broke down within months of his purchase. But on campus he always wore something with the Mercedes-Benz logo on it. He said, "It doesn't matter what I drive. I am a top-of-the-line brother." Years later when he finished school and was living in California, one of his friends from college happened to be in town and they got together for old time's sake. When the friend came to pick up his old school buddy, as they approached the car, he was driving a Mercedes 500 S. His friend from college said, "Man, you are doing well. You are finally driving a car that fits your name." But the young man responded, "No, what I drive finally caught up to who I have always been." His "in look" shaped his outlook, and his outlook created his outcome.

You can go anywhere from nowhere when you know who you are. Thank you, Lord, for taking the embarrassment out of Bethlehem beginnings and manger cradles. We thank you, Lord, for the renewal of our self image. We praise you, Lord, for a savior who has borne our griefs and carried our sorrows. We thank you, Lord, for permission and power to go all the way to excellence. We bless your holy name. No matter where we start or what kind of family tree we have, you hold us in the palm of your hands. We thank you, Lord for a way out of no way. We thank you, Lord for the joy of knowing that it does not yet appear.

GOOD-BYE TO GLORY

———✗———

I Samuel 4:22 (NKJV)

"And she said, 'The Glory has departed from Israel,' for the ark of God has been captured."

The incident in our text comes from a period of time of fear and frustration, difficulty and disappointment in the life of the people of God called Israel. The Ark of the Covenant, one of Israel's most precious and respected symbols, had fallen into enemy hands. The Ark of the Covenant was essentially a chest that held replicas of the tablets that Moses had received on Mount Sinai when God gave him the Ten Commandments. Some believed that it also contained the rod of Moses. The ark was made of shittim (acacia) wood, overlaid with gold, and having four rings into which carrying staves were inserted. The gold lid was known as the mercy seat, over which hovered two golden cherubims gazing downward toward the place where the Presence of the Lord was believed to dwell as he communicated with his people.

The Ark of the Covenant represented the very presence of God among God's people. The people of Israel had such faith in the ark that they sometimes carried it into battle believing that as they did, God was with them and therefore they could not be defeated.

This was what happened in the text: The Israelites had carried the Ark of the Covenant into one of their battles against the Philistines. When the Philistines recognized the ark's presence among the Israelites, they fought much harder against the people of God. The only way to defeat the devil—the ancient Philistine enemy and adversary of our soul—is by defeating the devil. Not debating him, playing with him, catering to him, trying to avoid him, not hoping he will leave you alone, but by beating him. The devil will not turn tail and run just because we join the church or because we become more prayerful or more spiritual. Increased spirituality means that the devil will war against us all the more. Even though the devil knows that his end is destruction, he will fight until the end because he knows some of the devil's most prized souls were those he corrupted at the end. Solomon was a wise and devoted king, but in his latter days he allowed his heart to be turned away from God. Judas was one of Jesus's most trusted disciples, but Satan got him at the end. Ananias and Sapphira were two of the church's leading members, but Satan got them at the end.

The philistines redoubled their fighting efforts, and this time they won the battle and captured the Ark of the Covenant. When the devil redoubles his efforts, we must redouble ours. We cannot rely on what we have done, how we have served or prayed or worked or worshipped, to sustain us when the devil redoubles his efforts. A Sunday morning worship, a ten-minute prayer in the morning, or a chapter or two from the Bible every day may sustain us during normal times but not when the devil has turned up the heat and has sent for reinforcements. We must increase in prayer as he increases in ploys. We must increase in the Word as he increases in his wiles. We must increase in determination as he increases in deviousness. We must increase in faith as he increases his fight. We must increase in getting up as he increases in tripping us up.

And there will be times when the devil will get the best of us. Read the Scriptures and you will discover that at some point the devil got the best of the strongest and the best; the Bible tells us that at some point on their faith journey, Abraham, the father of the faith, doubted and lied; Moses lost his temper; David plotted the death of one of his most conscientious followers; Elijah panicked, ran, and asked God to take his life; Esther was hesitant about interceding for her people; Jeremiah decided not to preach anymore; John the Baptist questioned whether Jesus was really the Messiah; Simon Peter denied his friendship with the Lord; and in Gethsemane even Jesus agonized in prayer: "My Father, if it be possible, let this cup pass from me."

Life is not some straight uphill journey from sinner to saint, from hell to heaven. Rather life is a winding road with ups and downs. Sometimes we get the best of the devil and life is full of glory. And sometimes the devil gets the best of us and life loses its glory. How do we face life when life has lost its glory? In the text, when the Ark of the Covenant was captured, the news was carried to Eli, the old priest who had cared for it. The tragic news from the battle was too much for the old man. Not only was the Ark captured but Eli's two sons, Hophni and Phinehas, were also killed in battle. Eli was able to withstand the news of the death of his two sons, but when he was told of the ark's capture he fell backward from his chair and broke his neck and died. Eli's son Phinehas had a pregnant wife who was near the time of delivery.

When she heard the news that the Ark of God was captured, and that her father-in-law and her husband were dead, she bowed down and gave birth, for her labor pains overwhelmed her. As she was about to die, the woman attending her said to her, "Do not be afraid, for you have borne a son." But she did not answer or give heed. She named the child Ichabod, meaning "the glory has departed from Israel," because the Ark of God had been captured and because of her father-in-law and her husband. She said, "The glory has departed from Israel, for the Ark of God has been captured." Today some mother or father knows how the wife of Phinehas must have felt. For them the glory of having no children have done some things to break their hearts. Today glory has gone for some woman or man who wished for a child and didn't have one, and may never have one. Today glory has gone for a husband or wife or lover whose relationship didn't work out. Today glory has gone for some worker or professional whose career never amounted to what that person thought it would. Today glory has gone for that young person who didn't make the team, didn't win the prize, or was not accepted by the group. Today glory has gone for some senior who feels that life has passed him or her by.

Today glory has gone for somebody who had a dream that seems unreachable when that person looks at the hurdles that still must be overcome. Today glory has gone for somebody whose health is under attack from sickness and disease. Today glory has gone for someone who has had to say good-bye to a loved one. Today glory has gone for some saint for whom the church has lost its thrill.

If you are one of those for whom the glory has gone or if the devil has gotten the best of you, there is a word from the Lord that I have for you. The glory may have gone, but love, hope, joy, peace, power, and perseverance can linger on. Phinehas's wife made one mistake—she equated the Ark of the Covenant, which represented the presence of God, with the very God that the ark only represented. The ark may have been captured, but God wasn't captured. The ark may have been in the enemy's hands, but God's presence never left God's people.

That's what we must always remember when the devil captures our children, our loved ones, our dreams. All is not over because God still lives. Sometimes the devil will capture our symbols, but he can't touch our Savior. Sometimes we will lose a battle, but the blood of Jesus still prevails. Sometimes he will corrupt the institutional church, but he cannot corrupt Christ. And sometimes preachers will mess up, but the prayers of the righteous avail much. Sometimes church members will fail you, but Christ's promises are always kept. Don't give up on your dreams or assume that a lost battle means a lost war or a setback means permanent failure—not as long as God lives to answer prayers, work miracles, and make ways out of no way.

As the wife of Phinehas died believing the glory had departed, so one day a king whose name was David would dance in the streets of Jerusalem because he was bringing the Ark of the Covenant back home. As there are some here today for whom the glory has departed, there are others who can testify that glory can return because God can restore what the devil took. God can restore glory. God can restore life, faith, hope, love, peace, and power that the devil took. Before you give up altogether, remember that God is still in the resurrecting, restoring, renewing business.

Not only can God restore what the devil captured, God can give you new glory. Centuries later an angel appeared to a humble maiden and told her she would bear a son. Even though no prophet had arisen in the land for more than four hundred years, and even though God's people were being oppressed by one of history's strongest powers, the Roman Empire, this child was not to be named Ichabod, meaning "the glory has departed." For God was about to do a new thing. So the child was to be named Jesus, for he would save his people from their sins.

By that time the Ark of the Covenant had been lost for centuries. But God had planned another symbol to eternally remind us that not only will God restore what the devil took but God will bathe it with new glory. For God took the same cross that the devil used to capture Jesus and gave it new glory. When Jesus arose after his crucifixion, he became our eternal reminder that God not only restores but gives new glory. Maybe you have made some mistakes and let some opportunities pass you by. God will not turn back the clock, but God will give what you have left—the life you have left, the time you have left—new glory.

Perhaps the devil has messed up your dreams. God can bestow new glory out of every setback and disappointment. Out of every trial and tribulation, look for new glory. In spite of ourselves, God can get the glory out of our lives. Despite the devil's tricks and snares, God can still get the glory out of our lives. Andre Crouch:

> How can I say thanks for the things you
> have done for me,
>
> Things so undeserved, yet you give to
> prove your love to me
>
> The voices of a million angels could not
> express my gratitude
>
> All that I am or ever hope to be I owe it all
> to thee
>
> To God be the glory, for the things he had
> done
>
> With his blood he has saved me, with his
> power he has raised me

To God be the glory for the things he has done.

Just let me live my life, let it be pleasing Lord to thee,

And should I gain any praise, let it go to Calvary.

With his blood he has saved me, with his power he has raised me

To God be the glory for the things he has done.

ALMOST MISSED ONE OF OUR GREATEST BLESSINGS

―――――∝―――――

Nehemiah 4:1 (1–6) (NRSV)

"Now when Sanballat heard that we were building the wall, he was angry and greatly enraged, and he mocked the Jews."

I n 1975 Steven Spielberg shocked America with his classic film *Jaws*. Following the story line of Peter Benchley's novel, a mammoth great white shark terrorized Amity, a fictional New England coastal village. Newspapers in 1975 reported an actual decline in beach tourism during the popular run of this movie. To this day, the bass tones of John Williams's score from the movie strike terror in the hearts of America's moviegoers. But 1975 passed, and we returned to the beaches. Then 1978 brought the return of the shark to poor Amity—"just when you thought it was safe to go back into the water," or so the ad for *Jaws 2* warned.

Something about the *Jaws* series rings true. I'm not thinking of great white sharks attacking humans—which happens but not often—but of the "just when you thought it was safe" motif. So often it seems that when our lives seem to be going well, disaster strikes. Take the hurricane that devastated Texas (Harvey), Hurricane Irma that ripped through Florida, and Hurricane Maria that tore up Puerto Rico. This is a reminder that just when you thought it was safe, something happens out of the ordinary. We experience God working in amazing ways. Then to top that off, we experienced a massive shooting in Las Vegas that is unlike anything we have ever seen in America. And these ups and downs are not limited to the national scene. One day we could receive news of the death of a friend, and just when you thought it was safe, a call comes that a love one is diagnosed with cancer.

Nehemiah knew the "just when I thought it was safe" syndrome all too well. Remember how everything was running along smoothly for him in the book of Nehemiah chapters 2 and 3. The king had blessed his venture and had provided supplies. The people had rallied around him and had begun to work energetically. Then Nehemiah experienced his version of *Jaws 2*. Suddenly in chapters 4–67 he is confronted with opposition, not only from his enemies but even from his own people. I have come to realize that into every transition God has built a mega-blessing. In every moment of decision, God has determined results that push forward the Kingdom. God is behind us, and God is pushing us. Where would the church be if we had responded positively to every one of God's "pushes"?

What would the walls of Jerusalem have looked like if Nehemiah had listened to the enemies and not to God?

Nehemiah's opponents, Sanballat and Tobiah, mocked the Jews in a voice that must have been full of animosity and spite. If they were living today, they might have said: "Who do these Jews think they're kidding? Be serious! They're going to rebuild the wall from all of that junk?"

Nehemiah knew who had his back, who guided his steps, and who prepared the table for him. Nehemiah could have missed the moment, missed the blessing. But this passage shows us that Nehemiah responded with a fervent prayer: "Oh God, get revenge on them! Let them be overthrown! Don't forgive their sins!" Now we must remember that this passage shows us how Nehemiah prayed, not necessarily how we should pray. It illustrates; it does not instruct. As Christians we are called to love our enemies. It shows us that when Nehemiah faced his worst, he turned to God. This is precisely what the Lord was trying to show Nehemiah and us in rebuilding the walls by focusing on our purpose, reviewing our practices, retooling our people, and reaching our potential. To understand what God is doing, and the task to which we have been called, we need to look behind the mask of the physical, the temporal, and even the intellectual and see the glory of God that was being revealed. How have we come to a point of missing our blessings.

I. We Missed The Moment And Mighty Blessing Because We Questioned The Packaging

Nehemiah thought it was safe to rebuild walls. He had not anticipated opposition and confrontation from his own people. The people were seeing the plan of God and the work of God unfold before their eyes. The Master intended for them to see it. This was his plan! I am so grateful for the things God intended for me to see. I never would have known them, but he exposed me to them. I have seen his wonders, his grace, his love, his understanding, his compassion, his faithfulness, and even his glory. He intended for me to see them. He has done the same for you.

Nehemiah had received his vision from God and was moving them ahead. Had they received his message to rebuild into their experience, things might have been different. But they did not like what he was doing, and so they questioned the package—"How can we do all this work?"— and the more Sanballat and Tobiah mocked the people, they almost missed their moment and their blessing. But Nehemiah went to God in prayer, and the word says his prayer was so powerful that it achieved its purpose because the workers continued to labor until the wall reached "half its height." In spite of insults from opposing leaders, "the people had a mind to work."

I am preaching this message because the church cannot afford to miss another moment. We play catch-up so much, causing the world to miss the splendor and the regality of our God. We are to move the world in God's direction. Too many of us are missing our moments, missing God"s moment. We are missing *kairos*, God's time, and all that is prepared for us, and instead of marching forward, we are crying at our rest stops. It is time to move! God told Moses to tell the children of Israel that they had stayed at the mountain too long, and it was time to take their journey. Some of us have been at the mountain too long, and we have not moved forward. I am preaching this message so you do not miss the purpose, you don't miss the opportunity to review your practices. God has sent what he is sending, but we missed it looking for something else. We cannot afford to miss our moments.

II. We Miss Our Moments When We Look For The Wrong Things

We miss the major move of God because we have missed the transition before the move. We miss the place of blessing because we have missed the transition to that blessing. Nehemiah was the transition, the herald, the announcer, but they missed the announcement because they listened to the enemies. They did not understand that God was moving and revealing his move through Nehemiah. And when the move came to fulfillment, they almost missed the blessing. Would to God that this does not have to repeat itself in our lives, but that does not seem to be the case. God moves, and we miss it because divine movement often is not packaged in a way that we can accept based on what we expect. You see, it is our expectations about people, things, and situations that block the way that God wants to deal with us. We have to have certain people in our lives. We have to work on certain jobs. We have to live in certain neighborhoods. Yet often God moves in a mysterious way. The Lord does not come in the manner that we expect yet still is moving on our behalf. We miss the moment waiting on things to be a certain way.

Nehemiah expected some opposition but not to the degree that he received it. So when he was mocked, he did not shoot back; he turned to God. Now I have to confess that in times of conflict and criticism, prayer does not always top my list of responses. How tempting it is to respond by plotting a counterattack, or to forget planning altogether and to launch into a defensive tirade. Nehemiah may have spoken in an unneighborly fashion, but at least he did so in conversation with God, not with Sanballat and Tobiah. All of us recognize that there are moments in our experience when we need to rely totally upon the grace and the goodness of God. There are times when we cannot rely upon our self-sufficiency. It is in these moments that we recognize we are not as independent as we think. We depend upon God because God is able to direct our paths and lead us in the way everlasting.

Thank God for the power of Prayer. Nehemiah was a praying man, or at least in this instance. Nehemiah responded to the report of the situation in Judah first by sitting down and weeping. The question was raised, "Did Nehemiah actually not know about the broken walls and the distressed society?" Perhaps Nehemiah heard old news from his Judean relatives, yet, for some reason, this time his heart was deeply moved by what he had known for years. Was God preparing Nehemiah for service by opening his heart in a new way?

I see a similar experience in many Christians today who know about the pain in the world but who live in a state of numbness. Then one day, old news pierces their hearts. They mourn over starving children in Somalia or people with a short supply of water and food after a hurricane. Nehemiah heard something new from Hanani and the others, but it may also have been that God prepared him to hear the "old" news in a new way.

Prayer can be a real eye-opener because it opens our eyes to the reality of God's presence in all of life's circumstances. Living life with an awareness of God's presence and providential care enables us to overcome the "midnight early morning tweets" in our nation. When we see God, it is impossible to see hopelessness, despair, gloom, and defeat. When we see God, enemies become less significant. When we see God, we see a way in the mist of steep mountains and low valleys. God's grace is greater than our sins, God's presence is greater than our fears, God's healing is greater than our sickness, and God's resurrection is greater than our death.

III. Finally We Must Be Spiritually Ready To Receive Our Blessings

Like Nehemiah, let us learn that God is big enough to hear prayers that authentically reveal our thoughts and emotions. After all was said and done, it certainly seems that Nehemiah's prayer response achieved its purpose because the workers continued to labor until the wall reached "half its height." I have come to tell you that if you want to build the walls of Grace through a purpose, look at your practices, retool the people so they can reach their potential, you must be spiritually prepared. In order to receive your moment, you have to become spiritually prepared. Too many of us are simply worldly prepared. We know our three R's and we have mastered our academic studies, but we have not invested time in our spiritual studies. The time has come for the people of God to become students of the Word and disciples of the spirit. We have to start making time for prayer and for the things of the spirit. We have to say to ourselves that knowing God is our utmost priority. You see, God has some unique ways of moving, and if we have not cultivated our spiritual understanding, then we will not understand divine activity in our lives. The Apostle Paul told the Corinthian Church, "The man without the Spirit does not accept the things that come from the Spirit of God, for they are foolishness to him, and he cannot understand them, because they are spiritually discerned."

It takes the Spirit of God to comprehend divine movement. Elijah realized that unless we are attuned, we will miss it:

> The Lord said, "Go out and stand on the mountain in the presence of the Lord, for the Lord is about to pass by." Then a great and powerful wind tore the mountains apart and shattered the rocks before the Lord, but the Lord was not in the wind. After the wind there was an earthquake, but the Lord was not in the earthquake. After the earthquake came a fire, but the Lord was

> not in the fire. And after the fire came a
> gentle whisper. When Elijah heard it, he
> pulled his cloak over his face and went out
> and stood at the mouth of the cave.

It was the Spirit that made Elijah aware. The packaging might have fooled him, but because he had cultivated a spiritual life, he knew the still-small voice. Your church may miss the moment because you are not spiritually prepared. We have to spend more time understanding and knowing the God who called cosmos out of chaos. You see, the better we understand our Creator, the better we understand how God operates, and how God operates through us.

We need to be able to recognize the voice and see the signs. We need to work at walking with the Lord so that we can seize the moment and be blessed. I must confess that I do not want to miss my blessing. I have been through too much already. I want to be able to lay hands on what God has put into my life. I want to know God, to understand God's ways, and to be ready for God's next move. I have seen some powerful moves of the Spirit already, and I must admit they have blown my mind. I do not want to miss the next one. I am praying and seeking the Lord more. I am listening more and letting God guide me more. I am reading more and believing more. I know that God is moving in our midst, and I want to see the transition and be ready for the fullness. I close by emphasizing, **DO NOT MISS IT BECAUSE IT IS TOO VALUABLE AND IT HAS BEEN PREPARED FOR YOU.** The world missed the Jesus movement, but thank

God there were some who had grown spiritual enough to realize that he was too powerful to have been destroyed on that cross. They gave up their ideas about the power of death and followed women to an empty tomb. They sought his face in the word in that upper room, and on Pentecost, the power fell down on them. They were ready, and God was working. Do not miss the Jesus move! He is moving right now. He is knocking on doors, offering salvation and pouring the power of his spirit. He is changing lives and creating wholeness. He is establishing relationships and reaffirming his Father's love. Don't miss it! Because it is all just for you.

Sermons on Growing in the Christian Faith

———————✕———————

Faith is the belief in the fulfillment of promises offered to you by that which concerns you most.

Faith is belief in the promises of achieving the highest good made by your God.

The many avenues by which our faith is expressed are symbols and, like road signs, always point to what lies ahead. Remember the encounter of Peter with Herod wherein the church prayed to God without ceasing. The result being that Peter was delivered from his chains.

God proved himself to be worthy of the faith of these few but also to be concerned with the smallest details of Peter's well-being. It was the church's faith as expressed through prayer and fasting that led to divine intervention in Peter's fate. Your faith can allow you to do that which seems impossible. Christ himself told us, "If you have faith the size of a mustard seed you can move mountains; if you have faith you can be heirs with him in the kingdom of heaven."

Just a little faith will enable you to lift your head above the turmoil of this world and bring you peace and strength to share with your brothers and sisters throughout the years. No matter the difficulty or hardship, I believe that by faith all things are possible. I know there is power in faith, and nothing the forces of man or the forces of Satan do can diminish it.

As you read these sermons on faith, consider he who died for our sins and how he endured shame and suffered so that God would forgive us our sins. Step out on faith! Time moves on and allows things to happen. This year step out on faith in God's promise believing he will make a way.

THE GLORY OF THE ORDINARY

---✣---

Luke 9:28–29 (NIV)

"About eight days after Jesus said this, he took Peter, John and James with him and went up onto a mountain to pray. As he was praying, the appearance of his face changed, and his clothes became as bright as a flash of lightning."

One of the most fascinating things to me about God is the specific purpose with which God orchestrates things. God has a predefined, preordained intention for everything, including each of our lives. Perhaps Jeremiah 1:5 says it best when God said, "Before I formed you in your mother's womb, I knew you." Yes, all of us have a particular design, a specific purpose, and a destiny God intended when he formed us.

Yet somehow God requires a level of energy and effort from us in order for us to maximize our God-ordained potential. What an interesting concept potential is. It is essentially a glorified *maybe*. Potential is the unfulfilled promise that lies

77

within you. It is what God intended for you. It is the unseen that sets the stage for what could take place in you.

Let me explain it this way: If you are anything like me, when you get in the driver's seat of a car you have never driven, one of the first things you do is observe the speedometer. You do this because in doing so you are able to discover exactly how fast the car is capable of going. But just because a speedometer says that the car can go 100 mph does not mean the car will ever reach 100 mph. It means the manufacturer designed the car so that it is capable of reaching 100 mph. It means that 100 mph is the car's potential. Whether the car actually reaches 100 mph will be determined by who is driving the car. If some of us are driving, the car will come a lot closer to its potential than if others of us are driving. But the potential of the car is the same no matter who is driving. And this is where a problem arises, because if we are honest with ourselves, there are moments when the seeds of skepticism and suspicion creep into our consciousness about God's design for our lives. Because as learned as you are, as anointed as you are, as sanctified as you are, as theologically astute as you are, if you're honest, the thought crosses your mind every now and then whether you are capable of doing what you've been called to do. And when you find yourself in this dilemma, something has to happen to convince you that your potential is worth reaching. Because in any sort of progress, there will inevitably be a measure of struggle. The interesting thing is that whatever convinces you that your potential is worth pursuing is inevitably the same something that sustains you while you are struggling to reach it.

That is exactly the place where we find Peter, James, and John in this text: looking for something to sustain them while they pursued the fulfillment of their potential and God's destiny for their lives. It was these three—Peter, James, and John—who formed the inner circle of the disciples. It was Peter, James, and John who were involved in some of the defining moments of Jesus's ministry. They observed some of the greatest miracles firsthand. They were with Jesus when he went to the Garden of Gethsemane. They were as close to Jesus as anyone. They were his boys, his aces, and his dear beloved friends. The curious thing about this episode is that there must have been people in and about town who had no idea who Jesus was, people who had not heard Jesus preach. Surely there were still people in the land who had not seen Jesus heal by the touch of his hand, people who did not know that the savior had come. Yet Jesus took people with whom he was familiar to the top of the mountain. In fact, Jesus took the three disciples closest to him to observe his glory. The question is, why did Jesus allow the inner circle—folks who presumably knew who Jesus was and what Jesus could do—to experience his glory?

The First Reason Jesus Allowed Peter, James, And John To Experience His Glory Was To Show Them He Was More Than Even They Understood Him To Be.

Peter, James, and John were of Jewish descent. The Jews were expecting a conquering king to be their savior. As a matter of fact, the Bible tells us that after observing the miracles, the Jews tried to make Jesus king. And Jesus's refusal of all the accolades was perplexing to them. The fact that Jesus didn't call down fire on the Samaritans when they rejected him was confusing. They were so enthralled in tradition that they could not imagine that the God of Israel would send a suffering servant to be their savior.

Isn't that just like us—trying to make God conform to what we think God ought to be and do? God is busy trying to bless you, and you are busy putting God in a box so you can be blessed when you want, how you want, and with what you want. But it's when we open ourselves to experience the fullness of God that he shows us his glory. It's when we are in a pinch that God is able to expose himself to us in a way he has never done before. It's not a matter of whether God is capable. The question is whether we are prepared to see his glory.

Many of us are like Moses when he met God at the burning bush. We have not experienced enough of God's capacity to know how to describe God. So when Moses asked God who he should tell Pharaoh had sent him, God said to tell him he was sent by **"I AM."** I like that because it's a description of the very essence of God. It means that God is entirely self-existent. Totally self-sufficient. It means that God is whatever you need God to be. Do you need God to be love? God says, **"I AM."** Do you need peace? God says, **"I AM."** Do you need provision? God says, **"I AM."** You can fill in the blank for yourself. Whatever you need, God says, **"I AM."**

That's the problem the intelligentsia has with God. The intelligentsia has a problem with anything that can't be fully understood. But God's existence transcends our understanding. God does not exist in time; God orchestrates time.

God is not a matter subject to proof or evidence; God is the standard by which truth is determined. That's why it doesn't matter how long you've been in church. There are some things about God that you just don't know yet. Paul says, "Now unto him who is able to do exceedingly abundantly above all you can ask or even think." God is more than just a car. God is more than just a house. God is more than just a rent payment. God is more than the clothes on your back and the food on your table. God is more than a bridge over troubled waters. When we really begin to understand God, we'll let God out of the box and let God be all God is. Jesus allowed Peter, James, and John to experience his glory to show them he was more than they understood him to be.

Second, Jesus Allowed The Inner Circle To Experience His Glory Because He Needed Them To Understand That There Would Be a Time When His Countenance Would Not Shine.

These three had been with Jesus during some of the lowest moments of his life. They had observed the unpleasant exchanges between Jesus and the Pharisees. They had sensed Jesus' sorrow when those who said they loved him rejected him. They sensed the pain in Jesus when he declared that the birds have nests and foxes have holes but the Son of Man has nowhere to lay his head. And it was in the midst of this miserable maze of experiences that Jesus took them on a mountain to pray. There, he showed them his glory.

I would imagine that part of the awe that these three experienced up on that mountain resulted from the fact that, while they saw a glorified Jesus up on the mountain, most of the time they had been with Jesus, his face had not been shining. This is ordinary time! While they were working in the field, while they were ministering in the streets, while they were doing the grunt work, Jesus's countenance was not shining.

We need to learn that while we are on the road toward reaching the potential that God has placed in each of us, there will be times when it seems as if God's countenance isn't shining. There will be times when it feels like God has left us alone. When it seems like God has abandoned us. When we think God has kicked us to the curb. You know that you're maturing in your relationship with God when you can't feel God but you know he's there.

It's like when you play peek-a-boo with a child. When you play peek-a-boo with an infant, you can cover your face with a napkin, and that infant will believe that you've disappeared. But as children grow older, they come to realize that even though they can't see your face, they can take their little finger and move the napkin to find you were there all the time. When you really get to know God, you embrace the fact that even when the circumstances suggest otherwise, even when darkness seems to mask his presence, when your senses tell you there's nowhere to go and there's nowhere to turn— when you don't have a friend and you can't find anyone to turn to—that's the moment that God is right by your side. Because God's presence isn't based on your feelings; it's based on your faith.

That's why you can have peace in the midst of your storm. That's what sustains you while you're trying to reach your potential. Even at midnight, you can sing with Paul and Silas that "He walks with me, and talks with me and tells me I am his own." You can rejoice even when it appears that God's face isn't shining. Jesus allowed the inner circle to experience his glory so they would know there would be times when they would not see the shining countenance of God.

But Finally, Notice Something The Text Says That Not Only Did The Inner Circle See a Transformed Jesus But They Also Saw a Transformed Moses And a Transformed Elijah. That's significant. You see Peter, James, and John understood that Jesus was different. But they could identify with Moses and Elijah. Moses and Elijah were ordinary, regular men, just like they were. Moses and Elijah had issues just like they had. They had heard about Moses and his stuttering problem. They had heard that Moses was a murderer but was still used by God. They had heard about a fearful Elijah who ran to find a hiding place even after God had given him victory. And yet there they were, up on the mountain with Jesus, appearing in glory. That's when Peter, James, and John understood that what you are now is only a glimpse of what you shall become.

When I accepted the appointment to come to Greensboro, I made my journey from Boston by myself. I made provisions and got on the Internet and Mapquest to plan my journey. The journey took me down Interstate 85 south. It was a long and tedious journey, some fourteen hours in a cramped car. I had no one to talk to but God. And as I was making that long and tedious journey, I could feel the weariness in my body and the fatigue tempting me to pull over. But what helped me is that they had signs on the side of the road that told me exactly how much farther I had to go to reach my destination. Every time I would see a sign, it told me that I was closer than I was before. I may not have been there yet, but I was headed in the right direction and I was closer than I used to be.

I know it's tough. I know you're struggling to fulfill your purpose. I know there are some doubters who question your vision. I know it seems that God has ignored your prayers. But every now and then God will give you a sign, a glimpse of glory, to let you know that you're headed in the right direction and you're closer than you used to be.

God has a plan for your life. It's yours! It has your name on it. Claim it. Walk in it. Live it. Celebrate it. Praise God for it. Thank God for it. Lucille Clifton, the renowned poet, has a captivating line in one of her poems that extends a marvelous invitation: "Come celebrate with me, for every day something has tried to kill me and failed."

Beloved! Let's celebrate! God has a plan for you. Open your eyes and look at all the Lord has done for you. Let's celebrate the blessings that are ours in the present moment. Let's celebrate the Lordship of Jesus Christ in our lives. Let us realize that because of his Lordship, we have future blessings in store.

SOUND FROM THE MULBERRY TREES

———✝———

2 Samuel 5:24 (17–25) (KJV)

"And let it be, when thou hearest the sound of a going in the tops of the mulberry trees, that then thou shalt bestir thyself; for then shalt the Lord go out before thee, to smite the host of the Philistines."

This simple story of one of the many encounters that Israel had with the Philistines is loaded with lessons of enduring value. It is also an interesting story to tell, lending itself to the imaginings of the storyteller. Permit us to add a few "could-bes" and "might-have-beens" as we share his exciting battle scene with you.

The moment that David was anointed King of Israel, he was a marked man. The Philistines immediately moved their army within striking distance. David did what we must all do when facing the enemy: he prayed. Samuel 5:19 reads, "And David inquired of the Lord saying, Shall I go up to the Philistines? Wilt thou deliver them into my hands? And the

Lord said unto David, Go up! for I will doubtless deliver the Philistines into thine hand." In other words, "Attack immediately! Catch them off guard!" This is a far cry from God's instructions when David went to him the second time.

After their first defeat, the Philistines decided to try again. The army was dispersed throughout the valley of Rephaim. Again David went to God for counsel. This time he was instructed to use a completely different strategy. He was not to launch a frontal attack as before. This time God said, "Thou shalt not go up." He was to move his army quietly around to the rear of the enemy and conceal themselves in the midst of some mulberry trees and wait.

I am sure that some of David's soldiers wondered why they tarried when it appeared that they could have successfully attacked the enemy right away. There are times when it is advantageous to move directly against the foe, and there are other times when it is best to wait and plan. The most important thing is to strike at an opportune time. Many defeats have followed haste. If God says wait, it is foolish to rush into conflict. Pastors have lost pulpits, and churches have lost good pastors because the wrong issue was brought up at the wrong time. God said wait, but the officers said, "Let us act now." And too often the Lord has not even been consulted.

The Israelites settled down behind the enemy and waited. What were they waiting for? David was waiting for a message from the Mulberry trees. God had told him to wait until he heard "the sound like marching feet in the tops of the mulberry trees, that then thou shalt bestire thyself." In other word the Lord was saying, "Wait until I get there."

Charles H. Heimsath suggests that, "Life yields her secrets and bestows her rewards, not to those who assault her by force, but to those who woo her with intelligence. We can wear ourselves out beating the air without plan or knowledge, or we can discipline and conserve our strength to useful purpose." God is saying to David that he has a plan and that he should wait until the strategy is made clear to him. It pays to listen to the whispers of God. The tragedy of our time is that we are either too busy to hear or we are not spiritually equipped to discern the voice of our Maker. We must be able to pick up "the still-small voice" if we are to eventually claim the victory. Many disasters have been avoided because some saint understood the accent of the Divine. It may not have been acknowledged in philosophical terms, but it all pointed in the same direction. "Something tells me" or "I have a feeling" are common expressions of being tuned in to Heaven's wavelength.

Waiting on God to come on the scene is a test of our patience and obedience. We know that he is omnipresent, but we consider him to have arrived when he manifests his presence. He makes himself known and his plans clear if we do not become impatient and act on our own. No doubt David was asked time and time again why they did not move into action. David would reply, "I'm waiting for my message from the mulberry trees." If Israel were to defeat the Philistines, divine instructions must be followed to the letter. The sound of marching in the treetops was the announcement that God had arrived.

I. God Always Comes On Time

God did not come on the scene empty-handed. He arrived with the assurance of victory for his people. The noise in the treetops was David's cue to arouse the men. He knew now that the Lord had gone out before them. "And David did so, as the Lord had commanded him; and smote the Philistines from Gibeon unto thou come to Gazer."

Wonders can be performed if we will but wait in the mulberry trees until the Lord is there to go before us. While Moses and the Israelites were praying from deliverance, God had already gone out before them and they did not know it. They had not recognized the message from the mulberry trees. Fearful that Pharaoh's army was in hot pursuit, blocked by the Red Sea, they almost missed the message. God had to tell Moses to remind them of the direction of their deliverance: "Speak unto the children of Israel, that they go forward." God often tells us to go forward in the face of what seems to be insurmountable obstacles. Whether it is the Red Sea, the walls of Jericho, or your personal problems, if our Lord says "Go forward," you go, and he will take care of the situation.

A man was expressing his faith in God to a fellow worker who was not so trusting. His friend said to him, "You know I believe that if God told you to run through that brick wall, you would try it." The man's reply was, "I surely would. If God tells me to run through a brick wall, it is up to me to run, and it is up to God to get me through." When the creator says go forward, the plans for your victory have already been laid out. When you get marching orders from the mulberry trees, bestir yourself, (KJ) move quickly (NIV), for God has gone on before you.

Sometimes all that is needed to carry out a divine plan is a sound. In this case, it was the wind in the mulberry trees sounding like a marching army that gave Israel the edge over her enemy. So it was when the early church was fearfully huddled in the upper room. "Suddenly a sound came from heaven like the rush of a mighty wind." We must be listening for sounds from heaven and be prepared to do what God is telling us to do.

In the book of Acts Peter is in prison and the church is in prayer for him, but they were not ready for him when he showed up as the answer to their prayers. How unfortunate it is that when God sends a message—through mulberry trees, in prison cells, in unfortunate situations—that we don't know what to do or how to deal with him. I'm telling you when you prepare for the incredible, you can be energized by expectancy and tailor your attitude and activities to anticipate what God will do. You should be prepared for the incredible when God moves in such a mighty way that you hear him shout through the mulberry trees: "Surprise!" Has God ever surprised you? Just when you were about to give up, God showed up and shouted, "Surprise!"

II. When God Leads, don't Lag Behind

When God goes before us, I suggest to you that you do not lag behind. No room must be left between our souls and our savior. Satan is waiting to fill the void with greed, jealousy, malice, and all manner of evil. There must be very little space between the sound in the mulberry trees and our getting up to follow our captain. Saul lagged behind and ended up falling upon his own sword. Judas lagged behind and ended up buried in a potter's field. The rich, young ruler lagged behind and left the very presence of salvation, still unsaved. Are you keeping up, or could it be that for some reason you are lagging behind? If you are not able to hear God's voice and it seems as though he is not hearing yours, check the distance between you and your God. It could be that a lag has developed and he is waiting for you to catch up.

It behooves us to stay close to him who knows the way. In the eighth chapter of Solomon's song, verse 5, the question is asked: "Who is this that cometh up from the wilderness, leaning upon his beloved?" This appears to be a prophetic look at the relationship between the church and her Christ. She comes out of a serious situation "leaning upon her beloved." This should be our posture as we travel through the terrible world. Leaning on the almighty ensures that we will not be found lagging. It is also our guarantee of a comforting companionship as we journey. "What a fellowship, What a joy divine, Leaning on the everlasting arms."

Four little words in this exciting episode of the conflict between Israel and the Philistines must not be overlooked: "And David did so" (II Sam 5:25). God gave his servant marching orders, and David obeyed. Obedience to the commands of the commander in chief is essential for a winning relationship between creator and his creation. One cannot fully obey until one becomes fully committed. In the pursuit of victory, we are often given rather strange orders. Joshua was told to march around the walls of Jericho seven times daily if he was to be victorious. An unusual way to fight a battle, but Joshua "did so" and walls were flattened. Gideon was told to reduce his forces if he would win the contest. And Gideon "did so." The enemy fled.

Many of us do not know that God is not just giving us assignments; he has a purpose, he wants a work done, and he is confident that we are capable. He will hold us accountable for the work assigned. God will hold us accountable for the blessings we should have received and the witness we should have made. He will empower, and he wants us to move on. We must not lag behind and give ground. We must sound the battle charge. A new day has dawned, a new hour has come, and the people of God have to rise to the challenge.

III. Finally, God Must Have Total And Complete Obedience

Procrastination can be dangerous and sometimes deadly. Delay has been the culprit in the loss of many battles. It can rob you of personal conquests. Moses almost missed his place in history because of his hesitation. Once Isaiah realized the divine plan and received angelic sanctions, he cried out, "Here am I; send me." Once the message from the mulberry trees has been made clear, we are expected to rise and obey.

There may be someone here today who is preparing for some sort of battle with the forces of evil. Satan has upset your home life or is causing you undue stress on the job. You are now ready for a showdown with those who are causing you problems. You have laid out your plan of attack. Let me ask you a question: Have you inquired of the Lord to determine his role in your next move? David did wait for the Lord to make his presence known. You do not have to settle the situation today. Wait for a message from the mulberry trees.

Before you take matters into your own hands, inquire of the Lord. Before you continue with that divorce proceeding, inquire of the Lord. Before you do bodily harm to those who have wronged you, inquire of the Lord. Ask God about the matter, and wait in the mulberry trees for your answer. Do not be in a hurry to move your membership because you are unhappy with the existing conditions. Do not rush into serious decisions without first inquiring of the Lord. It may take a little time in the mulberry trees before your marching orders come through, but you just wait until the Lord gets there. He's an on-time God!

God will come on time! God will come on the scene if you invite him to fight your battles for you. The battle is not yours!

I believe there is somebody out there who is not ashamed to turn matters over to God and you waited in your mulberry trees for an answer.

Somebody needs to become a standing witness to the truth that God can get the job done. Have your tried him? Did he deliver? Then come on and Praise him! Magnify the Lord with me! Lift him up with a joyful noise! Let the redeemed of the Lord say so!

> "Wait on the Lord, and be of good courage,
> and he shall strengthen thine heart. ...
> Wait I say, on the Lord." (Psalm 27:14)

To Retreat Is to Defeat

———— ⤫ ————

Matthew 9:17 (NIV)

"Neither do men pour new wine into old wineskins. If they do, the skins will burst, the wine will run out and the wineskins will be ruined. No, they pour new wine into new wineskins, and both are preserved."

The stage was set for one of the biggest battles in the history of the world. It was to be a major victory for Christendom and all of the followers of Christ. The year was 1519, and the great conquistador Hernando Cortes and five hundred of his men had just landed at Vera Cruz, Mexico, one of the strongholds of the Aztec people. As he addressed his men with the final pep talk before the battle ensued, he noticed that the men were terrified. They looked as if they wanted to retreat; they looked as if they wanted to throw in the towel and give up. The months of the long and arduous trip did not matter now, and the fact that they were running low on supplies was not even important. Fear had paralyzed them. They were standing between where they had come from and where they were going, believing that their best was behind them.

Seeing this, without thought, in an act of desperation Cortez gave a terrifying command. "Burn the ships, Burn the ships!" he shouted. He commanded that the ships that had just brought them from Spain be burned. He told his men to torch their only mode of transportation, and thereby ruined any possibility of retreat, any chance of going back.

You see he had arrived at a place where retreat was not an option. He now embodied the belief that what was ahead was better than what was behind him. I mean, when he looked at their situation, he saw the antagonistic Aztecs ahead, but he also considered the stormy sea behind. He saw the disease and poisonous water of the New World out of his windshield, while his rearview mirror reflected the despair of the Old World. In that moment he realized that what was behind him was his history and what was ahead of him was a mystery. And so, with a confident uncertainty, he yelled, "Burn the Ships!" He had reached and personified the point of no return.

Have you ever been there? Have you ever been at the place where you are just tired of the status quo? I mean you are so tired of how things are and have been that you would do anything to be a part of something new, something exciting, something fresh? You are unsure of what is coming, but you are sure that it must be better than what has been. Have you ever been to that place—the point of no return?

Has your marriage ever reached a place where you long for newness in the relationship? I mean, you love who you are with but things seem stagnant and you desperately want the fire to be reignited. Has your singleness ever put you in a position where you needed freshness? Has your career, financial situation, or even your educational pursuits ever seemed dead-end and run-of-the-mill? Has it all become boring?

Still not close enough? Let me zoom in one more time. In your church, your calling(s), or your ministry, have you ever found yourself dissatisfied? I mean, you are in service during praise and worship—in fact, you are the worship leader—but you find yourself longing for more. You are tired of the same old songs, the same old sermons, and the same old prayers? You are wishing, without telling anyone, that God would send something fresh. In the church it seems as if it's the same old people, at the same old meetings, asking the same old questions, fighting about the same old mess. It's the same old people, jumping with the same old shout, while hiding the same old sins. You ever been there? Have you ever been there in your mind, body, and soul, the place where you desperately need something new and where retreat is not an option? I need to ask you again, have you ever been to the point of no return?

Now if I were a betting man, I would wager that all of us have been there. In fact I would dare say that most of us, in some area of our lives, are there now. And let me hasten to say that I do not believe that our arrival at this is, in itself, a bad thing. The problem arises when, although we are at the point of no return, we want nothing more than to go back. We've become stagnant. We're stalled, we're stuck! We are too scared to go forward, so we stay right where we are, complaining and fighting about stuff that doesn't even matter. We are stranded on the sandbar of fear in the middle of the Sea of Endless Possibilities, and we do not know how to navigate. We are standing at the crossroads of life, where limit and possibility intersect, with a drop-dead decision deadline—yet we want nothing more than to go back.

We want to embrace the sunshine of new shores, but we also still want to chill out in the shade of tradition. We want the space of a newly constructed house, but we want the rent payment of a one-bedroom apartment. Am I bringing it close? We want to enjoy the conveniences of marriage, but we want the freeness of the single life. We want the accomplishment of owning our own business, but we want the comfort of a steady paycheck. We want the newness of a twenty-first-century ministry, but we still want to do things the way we've always done them. We want the future, but we won't let go of the past. Like Cortez's men, we are afraid to burn the ships. Let me hasten to say that I am not talking about totally doing away with the past. The rich history that we possess has helped make us what we are today. However, there is a big difference between allowing your past to inform you and allowing your past to impair you. For instance, anyone who has been trained to operate an automobile knows that when you put the car in drive to go forward, but look back—in twenty-first-century King James vernacular—ye shall crash. Drivers and passengers will testify that the windshield is much larger than the rearview mirror. This says to me that automobile manufacturers understand that when we desire to move forward, we need to see more of what is ahead of us than what is behind us. However, a rearview mirror is provided so that we are able to take an occasional momentary glimpse at where we have been, to get proper perspective on where we are going.

I am looking forward because that's where I am going. But every once in a while, when things get raggedy and ridiculous and rough, I look back in the rearview mirror of my life and begin to think things over, and I can see how far God has brought me. This gives me proper perspective concerning where I am headed. I can see the last time I thought my failures were bigger than my future. But I am moving ahead now. I can see in the mirror the last time that devil almost took me out. But he should have killed me when he had the chance, because I'm moving ahead now. I can see in the mirror the last time I thought God wasn't going to show up on time. But my God, my God. I am past that now. Let your past inform you, but don't let your past impair you.

In this Gospel text, Jesus is confronted by a few of the disciples of John the Baptist who were discussing the practice of fasting. Jesus is trying to explain to them that there are two different systems of belief going on: one was the old, the other was the new. In a real sense, Jesus is engaging them in a theological treatment of the power and purpose of prayer and fasting. He is teaching them that the former way they did things concerned only repentance, while the new way concerned repentance plus hope and liberation. Prior to this, they had fasted to be forgiven from sins. Now fasting was to deal not only with sin but also with the eminence of God and God's ability to change lives.

Jesus then imparts a story—a parable—in which he says, "You never put new wine into old wineskins; otherwise, the skins burst open, the wine spills, and the skins are ruined. You put new wine in new wineskins, and it's all good."

In ancient Palestine, the practice of bottling wine involved the use of animal skins. The winemaker would get a soft piece of animal hide and tie it off. He would then fill the skin with unfermented wine. During the fermentation process, the yeast in the brew would expand the soft skin until the skin became hard. By the time the new wine was ready, by the time it had become old wine, the new skin, which had been soft, had hardened and become an old skin that would be squeezed so that one could enjoy the good elixir.

Jesus paints this important picture to let us know two things that should excite us. The first is that he is talking about a process that new wine is going through. The wine is going through the fermentation process. Fermentation is a volatile process in which the wine itself goes through a metamorphosis. It becomes something that it was not by using something that it already had.

When the new wine is placed in an old wineskin, the fermentation process is impaired, but in the new skin, metamorphosis is possible. New wine has started to change, but it is not finished. It is in a state of becoming. You see, we all are in the process of becoming. You may not be what you ought to be, but you can thank God that you know how you used to be. I mean, things that used to make you mad don't really get to you anymore. Like new wine, you are still in a process. God is still working on you. What did Albertina

Walker say? "Please be patient with me, God is not through with me yet." I get excited about new wine because it speaks of the process and progress of becoming.

The second exciting aspect of new wine is that, no matter how you constrain it, new wine will rise. There is something in new wine that will rise in spite of how hard you try to constrain it. There is a yeast element in the new wine that under certain conditions rises in order to make the wine what it is supposed to be. It will rise even if it has to break the container that it is placed in. This is what Jesus shares about new wine in old wineskins. The old skins have lost their elasticity and would burst during the fermentation process. And I contend that those of us in here who are interested in becoming new have something in us that just keeps on rising.

No matter how people or the past try to keep us back, like new wine, we keep rising. In fact, we are so set on becoming that Maya Angelo's poem says it best: You may write me down in history with your bitter, twisted lies. "You may trod me in the very dirt. But still, like dust, I'll rise."

I'm reminded of the story of a toy that a little boy got one Christmas. It was a plastic boxing toy that had an interesting quality. When you hit the toy, it would fall but bounce right back up. No matter how hard the little boy hit the toy, it would keep bouncing back up. He invited his older and bigger friends over to take a swing at it, but the toy still had the same response. Perplexed, the boy asked his father why the toy would fall down but never stay down. The father smiled and said, "Son, when I put the toy together, I put something on the inside of it to ensure that no matter how hard it was hit, it would always bounce back up."

When God created us, when God put us together, God put something inside us so that when we get knocked down, we will always rise again. God put something in us that no matter how hard life hits us, we'll bounce back. That thing that God gave us, that thing that he put way down on the inside, is our ability to praise him. That will keep bringing us up time and time again. If this is new to you, try it. When they talk about you, praise God and see won't you bounce back. When they close the coffin on your dreams and try to bury them and you, praise God and see won't you bounce back. Relationship wrecked! Praise God and bounce back! Whatever it is that has you broken down, torn down, to the floor down, praise God and bounce back.

When I think of being guided by the wisdom, grace, and goodness of God, I am convinced that where I am going is better than where I have been. I know it's going to keep getting better. That's how walking with God is. Every round goes higher and higher—and higher and higher. I can't go back. I can't go back! "Forgetting those things which are behind and reaching forward to those things which are ahead, I press! I said I press! I press toward the goal for the prize of the upward call of God in Christ Jesus. I've reached the point of no return!"

We cannot know whether sickness or sorrow will be our fate, but our Lord has promised that he will guide us until the day is done. Somewhere and somehow in God's own time, the shadows must flee. Somewhere and somehow in God's own time, the load must lift and the clouds must rift. Somewhere and somehow in God's own time, we are going to reach the top of the mountain. Somewhere and Somehow there is a bright side; don't you rest until you find it. Somewhere and somehow in God's own time, we are going to see the king in the beauty of his holiness and the holiness of his beauty. Somewhere and somehow in God's own time, his will be done on earth as it is in heaven.

Preparing for God's Favor

---⟨✕⟩---

Genesis 12: 1, 2 (1–9) (The Msg)

*"God told Abram: Leave your country, your family,
and your father's home for a land that I will show
you. I'll make you a great nation and bless you.
I'll make you famous; you'll be a blessing."*

Introduction

Allow me to introduce Abram. He is a man who has been born into a place and position of riches and abundance. His father is a pretty well-to-do man. With a successful father, most likely Abram believes that all of his opportunities and even his destiny are somehow linked to his father. God, however, sends a word that creates a moment for Abram to decide whether he will become the man he is supposed to be instead of being governed and guided by the legacy of his father. God says three things that I think we need to understand, or three things are done in this particular text that will help us understand the vitalness of becoming what God has ordained: (1) God wants to do something through you, (2) God wants to do something for you, and (3) God wants to do something to you.

What I've done is I have reversed the process. Really it should begin with "to you," then "for you," and then "through you." I'm going to reverse it so you can see regressive movement; then I will show you the progressive move of God upon your life. In verse 3 notice what the Lord says: "I will bless those who bless you, but I will curse those who curse you. Through you I will bless the nations." Of course God is referring to the impending presence of the supreme revelation known as Jesus Christ. God is saying to Abram, "Through your legacy and lineage will come the Son of God, who will be the clarifier of the desire and design of God for Humanity." Humanity will come to know and understand who God is because of the revelation that will come through the line and lineage of Abram. When God calls you to become a disciple, he gives you a responsibility of being someone he can use to make clearer who he is to the world. God has a desire for you to be a blessing to other people, meaning he wants to do something through you. Many of us miss this because we spend too much time trying to be blessed until we forget to be a blessing. We are not saved simply to occupy space and time. We are strategically positioned, equipped, and endowed with particular gifts so that the will and work of God will be achieved, the worship of God will be experienced, and the witness of God will be known. God has positioned you wherever you are so you can be a blessing to someone. You are a part of the kingdom, and because you are a part of the kingdom, you have a kingdom assignment.

We all have kingdom assignments, which means we have been uniquely positioned to be a blessing to someone else. If we do not understand our kingdom responsibilities, we will go about our life missing the opportunities that God has for us. Far too many of us are too involved in our own lives to be utilized to the full extent that God has ordained for our lives. God wants to bless someone through you. God wants the world to know him better because of you. He wants you to be a kingdom resident and a kingdom instrument, someone who transmits and vocalizes the personality and Spirit of God to make a difference in the world. He has ordained that you be an influence in the world.

God wants people to see you and desire what you have and yearn insatiably to be like you. You are to be a model, a paragon, an example. He doesn't want you staggering around and meandering with no destiny, no purpose, no joy, no excitement, no enthusiasm, half-hearted, half living, or half struggling. *No!* God says, "I have created you with destiny and purpose because you are my child. I made you uniquely. You are wonderfully and beautifully made." I put in you something that gives you the ability to influence your atmosphere and to change, alter, and transform the behavioral patterns around you. You should not be walking around being influenced; you should be influencing. You should be the one making the difference because you have been created for greatness. God's favor is upon you so great that you have to start thinking of your kingdom responsibility. We have to start thinking in terms of kingdom influence. It is a sad thing we need the politicians, the government, and all of these supposedly important people to make us feel good about ourselves.

I. God Wants To do Something Through You

The reality is: We are the body of Christ. We have been uniquely endowed with the power of the Holy Spirit and what we say will happen. If we speak to a mountain, it will be moved—if we have the faith of the size of a grain of mustard seed. You have to understand your influence. You can't walk around feeling sorry for yourself because you are challenged. You have to understand you are empowered by the Holy Spirit and you have victory in your hand. You have joy in your other hand and you have peace in your life. If you will just walk in your anointing—and stop walking in your addiction, depression, dysfunction, poverty, neediness, and loneliness—you can start walking in your power, joy, peace, righteousness, and anointing.

God is strategically positioning people who have a kingdom consciousness to become the influence. We are called to be the influence, which means saints should be strategically positioned in every dimension. Every area of human enterprise should be exposed to a kingdom perspective in every situation. Part of what we must begin to grasp in this church, and in every church in the country, is that we are the influence in the world. We are the head and not the tail. We have to stop acting cynical and uninspired—graduates who have no sense of enthusiasm, destiny, or motivation. No one should have to wake up in the morning and motivate you. You shouldn't need a cup of coffee to get you going. You shouldn't need a cigarette co calm your nerves. When I think of the goodness of Jesus, I don't need outside help to get me motivated because I am a kingdom resident. You have to understand that God's favor has strategically positioned the body of Christ, in every aspect of human enterprise, so that we can effect change. He wants us to be a blessing. He wants us to be empowered people who can operate in political circles with a kingdom perspective.

You do understand that the king of Israel was a political figure who had religious or spiritual goals and aspirations. If you are working in the banking community, you should be able to bring a kingdom perspective to the banking community. In the process, you should be linking the kingdom to the banking community to access funds to achieve kingdom purposes. If you are involved in any level of commerce or at a corporation, you should be able to influence the information of the systems you are in; you should employ that information to promote kingdom purposes so that the corporation will be converted.

You see, half the problem is that saints get closet-like when they go to work. You go to work and your employer tells you "not" to read your Bible and "not" to talk about the Lord. You should just tell him or her, "If it had not been for the Lord, I wouldn't have this job. If I hold my peace, nobody will have my joy." You are on that job to bring Jesus to that desk and to that business. Every time you walk the streets, the neighbors feel the anointing. Every time you clean that building, you should leave an anointing all over the floors. Every time you sit at your desk, somebody should know that you have been in the presence of the Lord. When you operate in covenant and promise, God's going to do something. As he is doing something through you, you are going to effect change. Things are going to be altered because of your presence. Someone is going to pick up something in you. You are graduates and you are favored by God to effect change.

We don't have any business lacking influence when we operate under God's favor. The Lord said, "I have you where you are so you will be a blessing, and through you people are going to come to know that which will bless them." The word "bless" here has to do with being abundantly advanced. The Lord is saying, "When folks start fooling around with you, their lives are going to be advanced." You become an instrument that blesses other people to the point that they are better because they have been fooling around with you. Don't you want to be the kind of person that people say they are better because they know you?

Through you, God wants to advance others so they will come to walk in the fullness of everything God has ordained for them. If God positions you, he positions you with the intent of having influence. How many of you are operating in the influence of the kingdom where you are positioned? That's what you need to be concerned about instead of worrying about when you will get promoted or who likes you.

Because you are saved, there will be some there who are appointed to pick on you. There are some demons assigned to you. They show up right before you get to work, home, or school. That's why you have to be prayed up on your way. Every time one shows up, think about how good last Sunday's service was. Then fight on in the name of Jesus.

II. The Bible Says Through You, God's Going To Do Something For You:

"I will bless you and make your name famous." If through you God is going to bless nations, then you have to be at a level to be a blessing beyond you. To be blessed is a condition of existence and to be a blessing is an action. You are a blessing because you are blessed. When you are blessed, you can't help but be a blessing because now you have everything to be what you have been called to be. If God's going to bless others through you, he has to promote you to a place where you become a model of blessings so people can have something to look at. Some of you need to stop looking poor just to be friends with poor folks. Some of you need to stop acting ghetto just to be friends with ghetto folks.

The reality is you have been called to be a blessing. Now if you have been called to be a blessing that means the Lord's got to advance you beyond where you are. Whoever God wants you to bless can't be beyond you. So that means God has to push you ahead of them so you can reach back and bring them to where you are. Now if God is blessing people through you, then you are going to get the residual from the blessing. Do you understand that God is ready to bless you based upon your willingness to be a blessing to someone? "Whatsoever a man soweth, that shall he also reap." That means you have to begin to embrace the fact that everything in your life is a kingdom assignment and instrument.

Everything in your life—every pain, sorrow, piece of money, child—is a kingdom assignment and instrument. If you can understand that God has positioned you to be a blessing to people, then you can begin to recognize that in order for you to be a blessing you have got to be blessed. "To be blessed" means God has to move you to higher levels of abundance and prosperity. In order to do that, God will put you in a situation where by your own might you can't do it, but you will get there and do it anyway. Many of you are getting ready to get a promotion that you can't handle, but God's going to give it to you. Then God's going to promote you by blessing you when you get the promotion. Many of you are about to get a job that you cannot do; but because of the favor of God, he is going to give it to you, then use you when you get there. You have the favor of God over your life. Your appointed time has come! This is your finest hour!

III. God Wants To Do Something To You

God says, "I'm getting ready to raise you because you are my child. I know you have been through it, but when you have been tried in this fire, you shall come forth. It is not by night, nor by power, but by my spirit, said the Lord of hosts." God's favor is getting ready to take you where no one can handle, not even you. If you stay in the will of the Lord, get ready to see God move. It may seem like it is not going to happen, but if you trust in the Lord and lean not unto your own understanding, he will bless you.

God's favor is elevating people in this house who are willing to come under obedience to the power of God. The things you are trying to get on your own and do by yourself, God will make the way. I have come today to tell you that if nobody else sees what you see, don't stop seeing! If nobody believes you can achieve, don't stop believing—and don't stop achieving! You have been preparing for this moment, and today is not the end but the beginning of greater things ahead! Press your way until all generations behind you are convinced that average is not an option. Press your way until the day is done! Press your way until you can say like the Apostle Paul, **"I press toward the mark for the prize of the high calling of God in Christ Jesus."** You are not pressing to be on top of the bottom, but the high calling is the top of the top. For every test, pass it! Every enemy, defeat it! Every lesson, learn it! Every opportunity, seize it! If you experience pain, endure it! Every privilege you get, honor it, and for every blessing, thank God for it.

As I prepare to take my seat, remember no matter what you accomplish from this day forward, say "Thank you!" For the tuition that was paid and for the A that was made, say "Thank you!" For the parents who brought you and for a school that taught you say "Thank you!" For all the nights that you had to cry and finally for the privilege of saying good-bye, say "Thank you!" The appointed time has come and God is moving in Zion like never before! God said, "If you trust me and be a blessing to whomever I tell you, I will bless you more than you can imagine." In the words of Martha Munzi: "It's a new season. It's a new day. Fresh anointing is flowing my way. It is a season of power and prosperity. It's a new season coming to me! It's a new season of power and prosperity for graduates. It's a new season coming to you! It's your time! It's your place! It's God's favor coming to you!"

NOTHING ELSE MATTERS

———— ∝ ————

Romans 8:31–32 (31–39) (NRSV)

"What then are we to say about these things?
If God is for us, who is against us? He who did not
withhold his own Son, but gave him up for all of us,
will he not with him also give us everything else?"

Introduction

Today Paul asks us to consider the fact that God is our greatest help! The question is, "If God is for us, who can be against us?" In other words, "Because God is for us, it doesn't matter who or what is against us." No one can take away your salvation. No one can take away your salvation. No one can shut off God's love for you or foil God's plan for you. If anyone were able to do any of those things, he or she would have to be greater than God himself. Even the powers of hell may set themselves against you, but they will not prevail. Why? Because God is greater and he is on your side! In his question, Paul is assuming a positive answer. If God be for us, then no one can be against us. If God be for us, nothing else matters.

The truth of the matter is we need to know that the rug will not be pulled from under us and whatever was pledged will come to pass. We want assurances that our blessings are not at the mercy of others and will not be snatched from us. We want to feel confident that the efforts of our enemies will not succeed. We want to be sure that the enemies within and without are not going to be victorious. We need someone who can support words with power and decisions with strength. It doesn't matter what is going on in us or around us; we need to know that God is with us and not against us. That God is for us and not our enemy. That God is on our side and not in cahoots with Satan. That God is real and not an illusion. That God is near and not far away. That God is faithful and not negligent.

What does Paul mean: no one or nothing can be against us? Paul says all of that without qualification, without equivocation, without hesitation, without reservation, and certainly without explanation. This great apostle to the nations declares this to us in this text and in this day and time when the world is falling apart and there's trouble everywhere. The world is in conflict. The whole economy of the world is going down. The world is threatened by terrorism. Jobs are disappearing, and there is more war than peace, more poverty than plenty, more grief than joy, more sickness than health, more uncertainty than security, more violence than safety, serenity, or sanity.

What do you mean, Paul, when you say no one is against us, that nothing is against us, that no one and no thing can be against us? Does that make sense to you? It doesn't to me. Not unless I think beyond rationality and get into some kind of theology or spirituality. Doesn't make sense to sit up here in this conference and be mindful of all the things that are wrong in the world and wrong with us and then haul off and say no one is against us. Is it honest to pretend that everything is wonderful?

In this world there are many problems to be solved, and we don't know where to begin. There are many questions to be answered. There are many sicknesses that ought to be treated, and we're running out of healthcare. Forty-five million people in American have no healthcare at all. High-handed sin is out there. It needs to be corrected, and yet we don't have enough repentance. There are enemies that need to be redeemed and restored, and we don't have enough love in our hearts to reach out to them. We're so confused because they're confused and don't know how to love.

Believe it or not—and you may not think it and may not have a dime in your pocket right now—but I'm looking at all absolutely affluent people. We are all absolutely affluent because we have more than is necessary for the basic sustenance of life. We've got food, shelter, clothing, healthcare, education, transportation. We are so committed to our luxuries that it does not bother us that the rest of the world does not have necessities. Very little is being transferred to the poorer nations.

The United Nations says that .07 percent of any nation's gross national product should be given to the underdeveloped nations of the world. Well, here's the record. Germany gives .035 percent. Japan gives .028 percent. Britain gives .048 percent. And the United States—the richest nation in the world—gives less than all. Reasonableness says that we are all murderers if we permit our affluence to cause billions of hungry people to die because we are not as knowledgeable as we could be, not as sensitive as we should be, not as involved as we would be if we took time out to thank God for all God has done for us and shared that provision with others. The duty to avoid killing is much easier to discharge than the duty to save human lives—actively and aggressively, in the moral sense of the term. And yet Paul says, "If God is for us, who can be against us?" What can be against us? No one, he says. And he doesn't explain it.

First Of All, Paul Acknowledges That God Is In Control Of All Things

We notice that in this lyrical and theologically celebrated song in Romans 8:31–39, there is little mention of anything that is negative at all. And you have to go to other scriptures to find more of an exploration of the negative aspects of life. And you have to go to 2 Corinthians, the sixth chapter and around the third verse and verses following, where Paul lets us know that he is not in denial of evil and trouble in the world. Paul does not ignore all the ills of his own soul, nor does he deny the troubles and injustices of the world.

In 2 Corinthians, the twelfth chapter and the seventh verse, Paul says that he had a rendezvous with God face-to-face in the third heaven—that heaven above the first heaven and above the second heaven. And he went all the way up there, and he says, "I heard things that I can't even speak about. I can't even describe these great revelations that I had in third heaven. But when I came back to earth, Satan was waiting for me at the foot of the ladder and said to me, 'So you've been sightseeing in Paradise, have you? Well, try this on for size.'" And he gave Paul a thorn in the flesh.

So Paul says, "I've got a thorn in the flesh and I prayed three times that God would take it out." I know that some folks say just name it and claim it. But Paul named it and he couldn't claim it. The thorn still stayed in his flesh. But one day in the midnight hour, he was visited by a strange presence. Jesus told him, "I'm not going to take it out. I can do more for you than take it out. I can show you something that you can't see until you suffer. I'm going to let it stay there so I can bless you by it and develop you in it and prosper you with it and strengthen you for it and encourage you through it, because my grace is sufficient for you." Paul said, "That's all right. I'll be content with it."

Do you think you're going back to your pulpits in some of these middle-class churches and preach a liberating prophetic gospel of social change? And do you think that your own members are going to like it? They'll call a meeting on you and you'll think that you don't have a friend in the world. But I want you to know:. Paul said that when those times come to you, God's grace is still sufficient. God is in control of the things that are against you. He is not going to let us go down in defeat. He knows his role in our struggle. God is in control of these things, and if God is for you even when you fail, nobody can be against you.

Second, Paul Tells Us In This Text That God Is Consistently Concerned With All Things That Happen To You

In this world you will have mountains you can't move and problems you can't solve. I don't care how successful you are; your success is still shot through with failure. You failed in something even though you succeeded in something else. Sometimes you succeed in business and fail in family. Success will not always define your life. You will learn not so much how to market success as to cope successfully with failure. It is with failure that you will spend most of your time and that I will spend most of my time. Can you deal successfully with failure? Perhaps there's no other success than knowing how to cope successfully with failure.

What are you going to do when those who are far less qualified than you go stammering up the greasy pole to the top while you are left standing looking up? What are you going to do when Mr. Right turns out to be Mr. Wrong and Miss Right turns out to be Miss Riot? What are you going to do when Ben Bernanke's bubble bursts and your stocks lose all their value? The late Peter Gomes said that the test of a person is not on the mountaintop of success but in the deep valley of defeat, where most ordinary people must spend most of their time.

The clincher in this, and the answer, is here. The point is not to deny failure but to work *in* failure and *through* failure and *despite* failure until we have turned failure into the success that comes to us—not by denying failure or avoiding failure but by learning in failure that God is consistently concerned about us and is still with us. That God never left us. That we cannot go from God's presence. That God is working on our behalf. We cannot flee from God's spirit! And when you put your trust in God, you will discover that God has already put more trust in you than you are able to put in God. God believes in you more than you believe in God. God believes in you more than you believe in yourself. God trusted you enough to make you. God loved you enough to save you. God owns you enough to give you a job to do, a problem to solve, a burden to bear, a test to stand. Failure is real, but God is more powerful. Failure is tough, but God is more powerful. Failure may hang around a long time, but God is greater and mightier and longer-lasting than any failure you can possibly experience.

I'm an elder now, but I have pastored people long enough to know them and can say to this conference that **if God is for you, he's more than what anyone can do against you. One of these days you're going to learn, as I have learned, not just to thank God for your successes, not just to thank God for your victories, not just to thank God for your popularity, not just to thank God because your pews are full and your plates are running over. But one of these days you're going to learn how to thank God for burdens. Thank God for your trials. Thank God for your troubles. Thank God for the storms he's brought you through.** "Through it all, through it all, I've learned to trust in Jesus, I've learned to trust in God."

Third And Finally, God Can Change All Things That Happen In Our Lives

Paul is speaking to us today. We musn not judge ourselves by our background or our circumstances. We must look at who we are and trust the power and presence of God in our lives to give us the victory. Many times we live off our defeat because we do not know how to allow the power of the Spirit to give us victory. We must not shackle ourselves because of our poor failures; God has and will give us the victory. In order to move in this power of the spirit, we must believe that he is at work in us. He will work through us even when we do not feel worthy.

Paul is encouraging us today to keep on preaching the word. It is not time to quit; it is time to face what we have always wanted to accomplish and know that God has equipped us to get there. Keep on trying to help somebody and teach somebody and lift somebody and bless somebody. If God is for you, nobody can be against you. When your enemies turn against you and become your emissaries, they will make you more famous than you would have been if you didn't have somebody talking about you and making you famous. Because when your enemies try to tear you down, God will build you up through your enemies' unpaid advertisement. For while some are hating on you, God will send somebody to help on you!

Even when we want to be against us, we cannot be against ourselves. God will take every drawback and every hard head and turn it into a blessing. Why is it that we cannot harm ourselves? Because God uses every adversity as a teachable moment to let us know that all things work together for good. All things are in God's hands. All things will help you on your way because God believes in us more than we believe in God.

So the text does not say, "If we are for God, no one can be against us" but "If God is for you." We have been saved by grace—not by our thoughts, not by our by faith. And look what we have from God: committed comfort, corrective chastisement, continuing comfort, certain change, constant contentment, and ceaseless celebration. If God be for us, who can be against us? We've got a friend above all friends. We've got bread in a starving land. We have hope in every situation. We have help in every generation. We have light in every midnight. We have life in every death. We have victory in every calamity. For those whom he foreknew, he also called. And those whom he called, he also justified. And those whom he justified, he also glorified. And those whom he glorified, he also sanctified. And those whom he sanctified, he also purified. And those whom he purified, he also beautified. And those whom he beautified, he also qualified.

The late Peter Gomes tells a story about a former professor at Princeton University, Dr. Ernest Gordon, who wrote a book about his captivity on the River Kwai during World War II. In that Japanese prison camp, Ernest Gordon said that he and his fellow British who were captives were initially very religious, reading their Bibles, praying, singing hymns, witnessing, and testifying to their faith, and hoping and expecting that God would reward them and fortify them for their faith by freeing them or at least mitigating their captivity. God didn't deliver, however, and the men became disillusioned and angry, and some even faithless. They gave up on the outward display of their faith, but after a while, Gordon says, the men, responding to the needs of their fellows—caring for them, protecting the weaker ones, and in some cases dying for one another—began to discern something of a spirit of God in their midst. It was not a revival of religion in the conventional sense but rather the discovery that religion was not what you believed but what you did for others when it seemed that you could do nothing at all. It was compassion that gave them their inner strength and it was from their inner strength that their compassion came.

What do you have to say? I have heard your complaints and how mean people are and how bad you're having it. But do you have any blessings? Can you tell somebody that if God is for you, he's more than the world against you? If God is for us, who can be against us? If God is on our side, what do we have to fear? Psalm 27:2,3 "When the wicked, even mine enemies and my foes, came upon me to eat up my flesh, they stumbled and fell. Though a host should encamp against me, my heart shall not fear; though war should rise against me, in this will I be confident". If God is for us, nothing else matters.

Can you tell somebody that if God is for you, he's more than the world against you? Nothing else matters because if God is for you, then "Greater than he that is in you than he that is in the world."

ORDER OUT OF CHAOS

---◁✕▷---

Genesis 1:1; Job 38:4

*"In the beginning God created the
heavens and the earth." (NLT)*

*"Where were you when I laid the
foundations of the earth?" (NLT)*

Scientists are explaining inner space. Within this
decade, molecular biologists hope to identify the specific location, content, and function of each gene in
the human genome. The potential uses of such information
are staggering. Scientists are also exploring outer space.
This very moment, space probes are collecting new data
about distant stars and planets in our solar system. Almost
daily, we expand our knowledge of places barely visible to
the human eye.

Our age of information is amassing an incredible storehouse of facts about the world around and within us. We
know more than we ever previously knew, but as awesome

Order Out of Chaos

as our knowledge is, facts alone will not answer all of our questions. Even identifying all of our genetic material will not equip us to know why we are here. Even traveling to the edge of the universe will not explain how it all began. We should not expect science to answer such questions.

The book of Genesis says, "In the beginning God created the heaven and the earth, the earth was formless and empty, and darkness covered the deep waters. And the Spirit of God was hovering over the surface of the waters." It says in contemporary testimony that God called this world into being out of nothing and gave it shape and order. The author does not claim to have been present when God brought order to chaos. Nor does the author even attempt to explain why God chose to bring light, land, and life into existence. Instead, the author declares that God was and is in charge of creation and that God considers creation good. The opening chapter of Genesis is not a statement of scientific fact. It is a statement of faith. The world in which the author lived surely had its share of problems. The author no doubt had ample unanswered questions. But none of that kept the author from gazing in wonder at the world and its people and believing that all of it and all of them belonged to God. It asserts that life derives its ultimate purpose and meaning from God. I marvel at the inspirational sermons of the old Negro preacher set down as poetry by James Weldon Johnson. One of his sermons is titled the Creation.

**"And God stepped out on space, And
he looked around and said: I'm lonely—**

124

I'll make me a world And as far as the eye of God could see darkness covered everything; blacker than a hundred midnights, down in a cypress swamp.

Then God smiled, and the light broke, and the darkness rolled up on one side

And the light stood shining on the other, and God said: That's Good!

Then God reached out and took the light in his hands and God rolled the light around in his hands, until he made the Sun; and he set that sun a-blazing in the heavens,

God gathered it up in a shining ball and flung it against the darkness, spangling the night with the moon and stars Then down between the darkness and the light he hurled the world; and God said, That's Good."

Science and faith begin at the same place: meaning-less, chaotic nothingness. To stand up in worship and say "I believe in God, the creator of heaven and earth" is to identify God as the creative force who brings creation out of chaos, beauty out of barrenness, light out of darkness, life out of nothingness. We believe that the spirit of God is that creative power who rends the dark emptiness with light and brings into being all that is. I believe in God the Father almighty, as an affirmation of faith. It is the beginning of the affirmation of our faith. But what are the implications of that affirmation for us? What difference does it make for us to say that God is the creator of heaven and earth, the one who brings order out of chaos?

We are affirming that behind the created order is a purposeful creator. In spite of our theoretical denials, we have spiritual experiences that cannot be explained in materialistic terms. At night when we look up at the stars that bedeck the heavens like swinging lanterns of eternity. For the moment we may think we see all, but something reminds us that we do not see the law of gravity that holds them there. We gaze at the architectural beauty of some impressive houses of God, but soon something reminds us that our eyes cannot behold that cathedral in its total reality. We have not seen within the mind of the architect who drew the blueprint. We can never see the love and the faith of the individuals whose sacrifices made the construction possible.

Looking at each other, we conclude that our perception of the physical body is a vision of all that we are. As you presently gaze at the pulpit and witness me preaching, you immediately conclude that you see me preaching or lead-ing worship. But then you are reminded that you see only my body, which in itself neither reasons nor thinks. You can never see the me that makes me, me, and I can never see the you that makes you, you. That invisible something we call personality is beyond our physical gaze. There must be a God to give human beings the mind that can begin to perceive the process of creation.

So we can affirm with the Psalmist, "When I consider your heavens, the work of your fingers. The moon and the stars which you have ordained. What is man that you are mindful of him, And the son of man that you visit him?" That's biblical faith. Faith that celebrates the power and purpose of the creator.

We must also affirm that God is the maker of heaven and earth and our limitation as humans. We are finite, human, bound by time and space, incomplete in our comprehension of the creation and the creator. The tiny amount we know is surrounded by the infinite mystery we can never fully comprehend. To believe in God as the maker of heaven and earth is to celebrate that mystery and to live with a sense of awe and wonder.

Do you remember how Job struggled with this? In the middle of his suffering, his well-intentioned, intelligent friends used all their wisdom, all the powers of logic to debate and try to explain the ways of God. After they had done their best and their worst, God finally came onto the stage. God did not directly answer any of the issues in the debate. He had no need to defend himself. God spoke in his own time and way. God came as God, speaking out of the whirlwind:

Where were you when I laid the foundations of the earth? Tell me, if you have understanding. Who determined its measurements? Surely you know! Or who stretched the line upon it? When the morning stars sang together, And all the sons of God shouted for joy? Have you commanded the morning since your days began, And caused the dawn to know its place. That it might take hold of the ends of the earth. And the wicked be shaken out of it? Have you comprehended the breadth of the earth? Tell me, if you know all this. Shall the one who contends with the Almighty correct him? He who rebukes God, let him answer it.

Job responded out of profound trust and faith: "Behold, I am vile. What shall I answer you? I lay my hand over my mouth. Once I have spoken, but I will not answer. Yes, twice, but I will proceed no further."

There are times when the most eloquent expression of faith is silence. To live by faith is to live with that sense of awe and wonder that stands in silence before the greatness of creation, to dance with the music that could only be heard at the dawn of creation.

There is something profound about being a part of God's creation. When I look at my own life and the life of the world around me, I know that I don't have to reach any farther than my own soul to experience chaos. Within my arm's reach are persons who experienced disorder, confusion, and nothingness. We all need that creative spirit who brings order and harmony out of chaos and disorder of life. The Apostle Paul said, "Anyone who is in Christ becomes a whole new creation. The old has passed away, the new has come."

The God who gave us new life can turn our lives around. "I believe," which means I trust, I love, I give myself to him. God's creative work goes on, and by the power of the spirit of God, you and I are invited to be part of it. Gardner C.

Taylor said in a message: "There is something about the image of God in all of us. There are strange stirrings and a pull toward the stars in me and in you. There is a part of us we cannot understand, something within us, if only we would listen, that raises us our heads and lifts up our hearts. We are God's own children made in his likeness. This is our birth right, and we shall find peace only when we claim it and live by its terms."

Works cited:

The words of Gardner Taylor, Vol 1 "The God in Us" P. 24–25 Judson Press, Valley Forge, 1999.

God's Trombones - James Weldon Johnson "The Creation" The Viking Press, New York,1955.

RECONNECTING THE FAMILY BACK TO GOD THROUGH THE POWER OF GRACE

———— ⤖ ————

Acts 4: 32–33 (KJV)

*"And the multitude of those who had believed
were of one heart and soul; neither did anyone
say that any of the things he possessed was
his own, but they had all things in common.
And with great power the apostles gave witness
to the resurrection of the Lord Jesus.
And great grace was upon them all."*

Introduction

Eugene Peterson asked the question in the forward of Larry Crabb's book *The Safest Place on Earth*, "Why is the spiritual community or the church high on so many people's list as a major spiritual problem?" One would automatically think that being a member of a church would put you in a spiritual community. Yet we are struggling to define and create such atmospheres where Jesus is Lord and the Spirit of God abides.

As a presiding elder, my heart aches as I look at the church today and look back to what I remember the church was like in my youth. I remember it being a spiritual community with like-minded friends, a family of brothers and sisters, enjoying one another's companionship on our way to heaven. This theme—Reconnecting the Family Back to God—suggests that our sense of community is eluding us and we are no longer a spiritual community but a disconnected community. Does the church you worship in resemble the church at Jerusalem? I mean the church as described in the text: one heart and one soul, and having all things in common. What I am finding is that the larger we become, the more difficult it is to form an authentic biblical community.

It seems to me that today we worship with people we don't know. We do not know their names, their stories, their faith journeys, their calling, gifts, or situations. And what is really disturbing is that we do not seem to care to know.

In order to appreciate where this idea of a close-knit church community originates, we must look at the early church found in the book of Acts to see how they lived and worshipped among each other. Luke presents in this text an ideal picture of this new community. They were rejoicing in the forgiveness of sins and the gift of the Spirit. They had submitted to baptism; and as they identified with Christ in baptism, they were now being raised with him to walk in the newness of life.

So they continued daily under the authoritative teaching of the apostles. Their apostolic fellowship found its expression in a number of practical ways, one of which was "the breaking of bread." Somehow the presence of God was revealed as each one shared in a common meal together. It was much like the meal that Jesus himself shared with the two on the road to Emmaus. Isn't it interesting that while they reflected over the recent events of the day, they did not recognize the stranger as Jesus until they sat down and broke bread with him? It seems that often the mystery of Christ is revealed in the breaking of bread.

I am concerned for the Christian community in the twenty-first century. For if we do not begin to see ourselves as constituent members in a localized body of believers, we are going to miss out on much of the richness and the essence of what it means to be Christian. To be Christian is not only to identify with Christ; it is also identification with others in the faith. As a matter of fact, the Bible says this: "If we walk in the light as he is in the light, we have fellowship with one another."

You and I cannot be the church in discord or in isolation. We cannot be the church in and of ourselves. We become the church as we participate in the worship of God together. This is important because the contemporary church is slowly losing the essence of what it means to be Christian, yoked together in a true fellowship of believers.

Too often we sit in worship hoping to receive a personal word from the preacher. We lift our hands to have a personal worship experience or to get a personal touch from God.

And we never tune our ears to hear what the Spirit is saying to us as a people, a nation, or a corporate assembly. We are slow to concern ourselves with the other people in our row or pew. If you and I are not concerned with the people sitting around us enough to speak and look them in the eyes so as to remember their names, we cannot be concerned with someone on the other side of the church or in the surrounding communities, and certainly not out in the world.

The essence of this Lukan narrative is best depicted in the repetitive use of the phrase "They had all things in common." Why is this? I believe that the author lets us in on the process and the formula as he explains for us the mind-set and the attitude of the people who made up this community. It's found here in Acts 4:32–33:

First, They Had Singleness Of Heart And Mind. They had "one heart" and "one soul." They were not divided; they continued daily in the apostle's doctrine and fellowship and in the breaking of bread and prayers. In a real sense, they were in partnership and they participated as members of a society with common goals and beliefs, such as enthusiasm for spreading the Gospel and living by faith. Remember, to be Christian is not only identification with Christ but it is identification with other Christians.

And I don't know about anyone else, but every now and then I need somebody to identify with me. I need to know that somebody else has been dealing with some of the same things that I have had to deal with this week. I don't like feeling that I'm the one who's had to get over some stuff. I need to know I'm not the only one who needed deliverance!

It's not even fun praising God all by myself! That's why the psalmist declares, "O magnify the Lord WITH me, and let us exalt his name TOGETHER." The psalmist also reminds us how good and pleasant it is for us to dwell together in unison. What is it like? "It's like the precious oil that runs down the head and beard of Aaron, even down to the skirts of his garment. It's like the dew of Hermon, descending upon the mountains of Zion; For there the Lord commands a blessing—even life forevermore." I believe that there are some blessings that can't be released until we operate with this type of unity. So we can't afford to get caught up in this postmodern age and lose the essence of what it means to be Christian.

We cannot come to church, sit in the row, and not be concerned about the person sitting next to us. No longer can we come in and out like we are shopping for religious goods and services, like we are coming to a spiritual Walmart! Then we say in our heart, "If this church doesn't have what I need, I'll just go down the street to the next church"—never concerning ourselves with one another or the larger community in general.

This church in the book of Acts was a concerned church. They were concerned about one another. Although it was about five thousand of them at the time, they worshipped with singleness of heart and attitude. They had one heart and one soul.

Second, They Shared Their Possessions As An Expression Of Their Stewardship.

It is clear from the text that "neither did anyone say that any of the things he possessed was his own." They had a vivid awareness that all they possessed was by steward-ship and not by ownership. It was on loan from God. They realized that everything they had was provided for them by the hand of God. Psalm 24 teaches us, "The earth is the Lord's and the fullness thereof; the world, and they that dwell therein." The earth is his. The sky is his. The cattle are his. "The silver and gold are mine," says the Lord.

When one lives with the understanding that all that he or she possesses belongs to God, you realize that God can call for it at any time he desires. You think of yourself as a conduit for the blessings of God. God said to Abraham, "I will bless you, and make you a blessing." We must see ourselves as a distribution center for the blessings of God. When I live with the understanding, I'm walking in a vivid awareness that my entire being belongs to God. I'm aware that it is God who has blessed me! It is God who has kept me! It is God who opens doors of opportunity for me!

Third, With Great Power They Gave Witness To the saving power of the resurrection.

The power they had received from the Holy Spirit enabled them to work miracles in the midst of the people. See, the early church had to prove and demonstrate the power of the Resurrection of Jesus Christ. They existed amid a culture that worshipped many deities. Here a god, there a god, everywhere there was a god. So the early church felt it necessary to prove that the God they served was the God who answered by fire—the one true God: Yahweh. Not only that, they had to prove that Jesus Christ was one with God.

Well, isn't that just like the world we live in today? We live in an age that is not "church-friendly." We live in a pluralistic society that calls wrong right and right wrong. Everybody is living and doing what is right in their own eyes. We live in an age when many people are being told that there are many roads that lead to heaven, and you can just pick the road that suits your fancy. And just as in the early church, what is going to convince this age is the presence of miracles and demonstrations of the gifts and power of God.

Well, this text says that there was a direct correlation between their generosity and their genuine love for one another and the great demonstration of power that accompanied their preaching of the Gospel of Jesus Christ. When they gave of themselves and gave of their resources and made sure that the needs of the body were taken care of, it released the apostles to preach with demonstrations and with power. Their message carried salvation and everlasting life to anyone who received it.

The word "power" here means effectiveness, and it means they preached with the ability to persuade hearts. They preached, and signs and wonders followed their ministry. We need this kind of preaching today. The type of preaching that will transform lives! The kind of preaching that will save men and women to get delivered from addictions. The kind of preaching that will save marriages. The kind of preaching that will convince our young people that finding Jesus is the best thing that can happen to them.

Finally, Luke assures us that the church was showered with the Grace of God.

The entire community experienced the presence and grace of God upon their lives. The word "grace" here suggests favor. The favor of God was remarkably shown to them all. They had great favor in the sight of the people. Their preaching was accompanied by good will and success. Their ministry claimed great victories, and the power of preaching Jesus greatly impressed the minds of people. They astonished, amazed, and made a lasting impact on all who observed their community. Was it their unity that served as a means of opening the hearts of the people? Maybe it was their genuine sharing and fellowship that assisted them in winning lost souls to Jesus. If we wish to win others to Christ, nothing does this better than showing others kindness, and even ministering to their physical needs.

Benevolence toward people softens their hearts and inclines them to listen to the gospel. It removes the blinders off their eyes such that they can see a living example of the love of Christ and opens their ears to hear the message of Christ. Jesus was constantly engaged in healing the diseased and supplying the needs of the people. He drew around him the poor, the needy, and the diseased, and supplied them to receive his message of truth. We too can have that same grace upon our lives. The favor of God is the benevolence of God. He daily loads us with benefits and blessings, mercy, and grace!

I'm tired of coming in and seeing certain pockets of people being blessed. I'm looking for the day when we come in the church and everybody has what they need! I'm looking for the day when my whole row is blessed! When no one is living in isolation and everyone has significant relationships and connections.

Oh, what a day, when everybody I come in contact with at this church—everyone's cup is running over with the blessings and benefits and favor of God! When great grace and favor and blessing are upon us all! When it's not just my house, but when your house is blessed! Not just my business, but your business is blessed! No just my children, but when your children are blessed! Anybody else looking for that day?

THE QUESTION FOR OUR TIME

------------✃------------

Mark 8:36 (NKJV)

"For what will it profit a man to gain the whole world and lose his own soul?"

I f we are honest, we will admit that sometimes we sabotage ourselves by seeking so-called success. We limit our own lives by trying to attain what appear to be assorted accoutrements of accomplishments. We become coconspirators in a plot to secure seeming satisfaction, not knowing that we have actually committed grand larceny against ourselves, stealing from the storehouse of our own souls. And to this behavior the Christ asks a question: "What will it profit you to gain the whole world and lose your soul?"

Let's go to the text and get the context out of which this question comes. After restoring sight to a blind man at Bethsaida, Jesus comes into the district of Caesarea Philippi. Caesarea Philippi housed the temple of white marble, which was built by Herod the Great to honor Caesar Augustus. Caesarea Philippi was littered with temples dedicated to

Baal worship. That's worship of idol gods, manmade gods. Kind of like temples and churches today that worship money and not the master. Temples that honor the gifts rather than the gift giver.

Caesarea Philippi was a military center of the mighty Roman Empire. The empire that took over others' lands in the name of establishing freedom. The empire that imposed Patriot Acts and COINTELPRO in order to shut up anyone who spoke against the empire. And so, into this place of prosperity and military might came a poor, peasant preacher-carpenter from Capernaum. Jesus called the crowd together and asked the rhetorical question, "What will it profit a man or woman to gain the whole world and lose their own soul?" This is a rhetorical question. Rhetorical questions don't necessarily require answers, but they can relay truth.

I want to submit to you that the genius of Jesus is shown in where and of whom he asked this question. Jesus asked this question to a people living under an empire. An empire that kept taking and taking land and everything else from other people. It was an empire that promoted prosperity for the privileged to the detriment of the poor. It was *the* Empire. So in a materialistic empire an individual may begin to think, "My purpose for being is to get, get, get, and take, take, take." So Jesus asks the question, "What will it profit you to get, get, get and lose who you are?"

By asking this question in this context, the first truth Jesus dealt with was the truth about possessions. What does it profit to gain the whole world and lose your soul? When you lose your soul, you lose yourself. Your soul is the essence of who you are. When you lose yourself, you lose the focus of being who God has created you to be. You then define yourself by that which is alien and outside of you rather than by that which is within you.

Through psychology, we can get a glimpse of why, in this empire, we focus on possession of things rather than possession of our full personhood. African psychology, then and now, deals with knowing the self. And the self for ancient and current Africans is the soul. The self is not what you do or how many letters you have behind your name. The self is not where you've been, what car you drive, or how many suits you have. Self is the real you. Behind all that materialism, who are you? Where do you come from? Where are your people from? When you take off the Saint John's, the Versace, or even your name brands, who are you? What is the substance of your being? When you look in the mirror, who do you see? When you are alone with just your thoughts, and your God, what's there?

Paul Lawrence Dunbar wrote in a poem, "We wear the mask that grins and lies, it hides our cheeks and shades our eyes, this debt we pay to human guile; with torn and bleeding hearts we smile." Dunbar's poem describes how we wear masks to hide who we really are. And if we are not careful, we'll wear the masks so well that we won't know our own selves. What will it profit you to get everything that is not you and lose you? What does it profit you to gain the whole world but have no ownership over who you really are? Jesus's question provides us wisdom concerning real possession. Real possession is not owning a lot of stuff; it is owning who and whose you really are.

But this question also deals with the truth about perspective. How do you see things? Please remember we are talking about Caesarea Philippi—the capital of the empire. And Jesus came into this capital of ancient capitalism and asked a question that relays a totally different worldview than what these people had heard before. The empire was saying, "Get." Jesus asked, "What will all that getting get you?" The empire was saying "Take." Jesus said, "All that taking won't take you anywhere in life." The empire was saying, "Steal from folks in order to pad your own pockets." Jesus said, "Give and it shall be given to you." The empire said, "Hold on to everything you can in life." Jesus said, "Those who want to save their life will lose it."

This rhetorical question is trying to convince us to change our perspective from getting to giving. Change your perspective from getting to giving. Change your perspective from valuing things outside of you to valuing yourself. God made a masterpiece when God made you. God breathed God's self into you. Change your perspective from trying to be like everyone else to bring the best self you can be.

Changing your perspective will change your priorities. When you perceive things differently, then different things become important to you. Your priorities change. Here was this poor, peasant preacher-carpenter from Capernaum talking to those who were the citizens of Caesar's empire. They too were victims of an economic system that made the rich richer on the backs of the poor, who kept getting poorer. Jesus came asking, "Is getting riches and wealth the most important thing in life to you?" Is that what you feel you are here for? Now, I'm not trying to get into your business about how much money you make. But some people define themselves by how much they make. Don't let money make you. Because if you let the money make you, Jesus says you are a rich fool. And the soul of the rich fool was required because he had misplaced priorities. When you get a sense of who you are, then your perspective will change. When your perspective changes, your priorities will change. And when your priorities change, then you will be able to fully embrace your purpose.

By asking this question, Jesus also let the people of the empire know that their purpose was not in getting all they could get, to the detriment of others and themselves. Your purpose is found inside you. You don't have to go looking for anyone else to tell you what you should do. Just look inside yourself, to the God within you. There is a marvelous scene in the movie *The Wiz*. And at the end of *The Wiz*, Dorothy, Scarecrow, Tin Man, and Lion find out that the so-called Wiz is a phony. They find out that the one to whom they thought they could go to get what they needed to survive, that person was actually searching for it himself.

Scarecrow asked for a brain. But when he was hanging on the pole singing, "You can't win," he was already reading bits of paper and literature written by great philosophers who said otherwise. Tin Man asked for a heart so he could love and feel. But throughout the whole story, he was crying at the drop of a hat. Lion asked for courage. But Lion was the one who saved them in the subway. So Dorothy had to tell them that they already had what they needed in order to proceed.

But then Lena Horne (who played the Good Witch) had to remind Dorothy of the same truth by explaining the concept of home to her. Lena said home is about knowing yourself and your purpose, so that regardless of where you are, you can always be at home. They didn't need a fake Wiz to tell them who they were because they had it in them all the time. The same is true for your God-given purpose in life.

But finally, this rhetorical question is still relevant for our times because it asks who has the real power. I have learned that there are two types of power. There is disabling power, and there is enabling power—and enabling power is the real power. Just because you have the power to take over lands and kill innocent men, women, and children, Mr. President, that doesn't mean that you have the real power. That's disabling power. Just because you can make laws in an empire that leave inner-city children behind but leave no millionaires behind, that doesn't mean you have real power. That's disabling power. Just because you had the Supreme Court help get you selected when you weren't elected, that doesn't mean you have the real power. That's disabling power.

But God has enabling power. For in Genesis, he took some dust and infused it with his divinity, and life blossomed. That's real power; it's enabling power. God parted the Sea of Reeds and let the redeemed cross over. That's real power; it's enabling power. But not only that; God put some sanctified semen into a teenage virgin, and she brought forth a baby born in a barn in Bethlehem. That's real power. That same baby grew up and turned tears to testimonies on Resurrection Sunday. That's real power. I'm talking about a God created my salvation. **"A God who took raw chaos and verified Descartes's intuition. Magnified Hegel's law. Clarified Plato's idea. Satisfied Socrates's question. Purified Kant's categories. Justified Abraham's faith. Gratified Amos's justice. Fortified Hosea's love. Sanctified Micah's mercy. Beautified Ezekiel's vision. Edified Job's confidence. Glorified the whole creation."** That's power. It's that power that saved my soul. Hallelujah! And that's all the power you need tonight. Power! Power! Power!

Works cited

Adams, Charles G. 9.11.01 African American Leaders respond to an American Tragedy. "Meeting God Again, the First Time: Judson Press, Valley Forge, 2001. quote on pg 149.

A MOTHER'S REQUEST

---◁×---

Matthew 20:20–23

Faith is only faith when it has learned to accept the no's as well as the yeses of God. This was a lesson that all the disciples who walked with Jesus had to learn. This was a lesson that Paul, who counted all things as lost for the sake of Christ, had to learn. This was a lesson that Jesus learned as he agonized in the Garden of Gethsemane about the necessity of the cross. This is a lesson that each of us must learn if we intend to follow Jesus to the end.

This was a lesson that Salome had to learn on her own faith journey. Salome has the distinction of being the only woman in the Gospels whose request was denied by Jesus. In the Gospels, whenever a woman made a request of Jesus, he usually complied. When Jesus's mother asked him to intercede for a young couple whose wine had run out at their wedding feast, he complied. He may have been irked because his mother was disregarding his timetable, but he did what she asked nevertheless. When Martha and Mary sent for him to come see about their brother Lazarus, he came. He may have been late according to their standards, but he came nevertheless. When the Syrophenician woman brought her sick daughter to him to be healed, he granted her request. His first response may have seemed cold, but he did what she wanted nonetheless. When mothers brought young children to Jesus to bless them, he did so despite the misguided efforts of his well-intentioned disciples to shield him from those who might have disturbed him. When the woman with an issue of blood touched his garment to be healed, Jesus responded to her unspoken request and ameliorated her condition. In the Gospels, whatever women sought from the Lord, they usually received. Yet he turned down the request of Salome.

Jesus's no to Salome is significant when one considers who she was. The Gospel of Matthew identifies her as one of the women, along with Mary Magdalene, who had followed Jesus from Galilee and had ministered to him. Thus, she was one of his loyal supporters, and as the wife of Zebedee, who owned a flourishing fishing business, she was undoubtedly one of his strong financial backers. There is a tradition that believes Salome was the sister of Mary, Jesus's mother; if that is true, then she was Jesus's aunt. As his Aunt, she had probably known him all his life; she may have even cared for him when he was an infant. Thus, when she spoke, she did so from the perspective of strong and close family ties. Whether she was actually Jesus's aunt or not, she was in fact the mother of James and John, two of the Lord's closest and most prominent disciples. She was a person with political and personal clout among the disciples, yet Jesus told her no.

The response of Jesus is significant when one looks at the way in which she came to Jesus. According to Scripture, she knelt before him; she came humbly. She didn't come to Jesus demanding anything because she was one of his supporters. She didn't come to Jesus claiming any rights due her because she was his senior. She didn't come trying to lay a guilt trip on the Master because she was his aunt or because he had deprived her of the two sons who one day might be needed to take care of her. She came to him humbly; she came with the right attitude and spirit, yet Jesus told her no.

I. The Nature of Jesus is significant when one considers the nature of her request

Essentially she was not asking anything for herself; she was interceding for others. Her request reflected the spirit of Christ, who was always giving. We often talk about the cost of discipleship and what is required of us to be Christians. We often refer to the fact that we are called to take up crosses. However, let us not forget that Jesus is essentially a giver. He gives much more that he receives and returns much more than he keeps. When he asks for something, he does so not to receive but that we might be blessed even as we give. With all the charges and accusations the enemies of Jesus brought against him, no one accused him of taking or keeping anything for himself. Whatever he received he gave back to them. When he received a little boy's lunch, he gave back a banquet for five thousand persons. When he received words of praise, he gave them back as praise to his heavenly father. When he received bread and wine, he gave it to his disciples and us as symbols of their redemption.

Jesus was essentially a giver, and so was Salome. She gave her time to minister to Jesus, and her sons to be his disciples. Her husband, Zebedee, was not getting any younger. She could have resisted the call of James and John to become disciples of Jesus. Salome did not put any hindrances in the way of her sons' calling but became a follower of Jesus herself. She gave of her substance, and she gave of the most prized possession that any true mother has—she gave her sons to Jesus. On bended knees with her two sons, she came to him and said, "Master, I have something to ask of you for these two sons of mine who are already close to you and whom you have already taken into your confidence on more than one occasion. Command that one may sit on your right hand and the other on your left."

II. Their request showed an audacious leap of faith

Now before we criticize Salome for her question\request, let us observe that there is nothing wrong per se with a mother looking out for the best interests of her children. What good parent doesn't want a better life for his or her children? Good parents are not envious of their children's successes. Good parents hope that their children will go further in life than they have, and if they can do anything to pave the way to help them, they will. Salome in her request was only looking out for the well-being of her children as any good mother should- yet Jesus told her no.

Let us further note that there is nothing wrong per se with the desire to be next to Jesus in the kingdom that he will establish. Salome and her sons are to be commended for believing in a penniless, weaponless preacher whom they followed to bring a kingdom into being. Their request showed an audacious leap of faith. Jesus recognized that although Salome's faith was well-intentioned, it had much to learn. He said, "You don't know what you are asking. Are you able to drink the cup that I am to drink?" They said to him, "We are able." He said, "You will drink my cup, but to sit at my right hand and my left hand is not mine to grant; it is for those whom it has been prepared."

III. Before we can fully enter the kingdom, there are some cups from which faith must drink, some of which can be bitter

Our inclination is to ask God to remove the bitter cups from our lives. Sometimes God says no to us because those cups qualify us to enter the kingdom of God. I once knew a lady of great faith who constantly prayed for healing. Her healing never came, but she had such a sweet disposition and such faith that she encouraged everyone who met her. I don't deny that her cup was bitter, but the fact that she drank it well allowed her to enter into the kingdom.

It is said that a monk prayed that he might have the marks of the Lord upon his hands and feet. He had a dream in which he saw a mark on the Lord's body that the world had forgotten. It was the mark upon his shoulder made by the cross as he bore it to Calvary. The monk discovered that he could only have the marks of the Lord on his hands and feet if he had the marks on the shoulder that come from bearing the cross.

If we do not drink of certain cups, then we lose the key to the kingdom for which our faith unlocks the door. If we do not drink from certain cups, then we cancel our reservations on the journey that leads from earth to heaven and from time to eternity. It is only as we drink from certain cups that we enter the kingdom. It was only as Charlotte Elliott drank from the cup of illness that she wrote her hymn of commitment, "Just as I am without one plea." It was only as Charles Wesley drank from the cup of persecution that he wrote "Jesus, Lover of my Soul." It was only as John Newton drank from the cup of remorse over his involvement in slavery and the wonder of salvation that he wrote "Amazing Grace." It was only as Fanny Crosby drank from the cup of blindness that she wrote, "Blessed Assurance." It was only as Elisha Hoffman drank from the cup of ministering to the distressed and brokenhearted that he wrote **"I must tell Jesus"** It was only as blind George Matheson drank from the cup of a jilted lover that he wrote, **"O love that will not let me go."** It was only as Thomas Dorsey drank from the cup of sorrow as he mourned the passing of his wife that he wrote "Precious Lord, Take my Hand."

Perhaps Jesus gave Salome a further explanation:

> You and your sons shall drink of my
> cup. James will be among the first of my
> disciples to be martyred for the cause of
> the kingdom. John will live to be an old
> man, but he shall experience persecution,
> banishment, and distress. He will see all
> of his companions die one by one until in
> extreme old age he will be left alone on
> a Isle called Patmos writing the book of
> revelation. As their mother and as a loyal
> follower, you will have your share of the
> cup of sorrow, but I still must say no to
> your request. To sit at my right hand and
> my left hand is not mine to grant, but it is
> for those for whom it has been prepared
> by my Father.

Jesus could have added:

> If I say yes to you, I'll have to say no to too
> many people. If I say yes to you, I'll have
> to say no to too many Christians who will
> come after you, who will face raging lions
> and be burned at the stake, and who will
> have as much right to those places as you.
> If I say yes to you, then I'll have to say no
> to faithful men and women who will stand

by the church for years, who will struggle
to keep the doors open in lean years.

I'm glad Jesus said no to Salome because then he was
able to say yes to another host. John, the Revelator wrote
about it: (Revelation 7: 9,13,14,16)

> After this I looked, and behold a great
> multitude which no man could number,
> from every nation, from all tribes and
> peoples and tongues, standing before
> the throne and before the lamb. And the
> elders will say, Who are these, clothed in
> white robes, and whence come they, and
> he said to me, These are they who have
> come up out of great tribulation, they have
> washed their robes and made them white
> in the blood of the lamb.

> They shall hunger no more, neither shall
> they thirst anymore, For the lamb in the
> midst of the throne will be their shepherd,
> and he will guide them to springs of living
> water.

SERMONS SEEKING GOD'S SPIRIT FOR RENEWAL

———————⊃⊂———————

What does it mean to be filled with the Holy Spirit? It means, first of all, to recognize with the Psalmist, "O Lord, how manifold are your works! In wisdom you have made them all ... living things both small and great" (Psalm 104:24–25). It means to recognize that we are in this world but not of this world.

To be filled with the Holy Spirit is to speak each other's language. It is to pray for each other's well-being until there is no skin left on our knees. It is to yield to sympathy. It is to love, not blame, to compete only when appropriate.

Pentecost is widely considered the birthday of the church. That's important, for if it is the coming of the Spirit that marks the beginning of the Christian church, then to Christians it is the Spirit that counts. Love is everything; all the rest is commentary.

So I pray God that through these messages the Holy Spirit may fill your hearts daily to accept our acceptance. May the passion of Pentecost persuade us all to rejoice and teach us how to praise.

WHEN GOD'S PEOPLE NEED A FRESH SPIRIT

---✕---

John 7:37–38 (NRSV)

"On the last day of the festival, the great day, while Jesus was standing there, he cried out, Let anyone who is thirsty come to me, and let the one who believes in me drink. As the scripture has said, Out of the believers heart shall flow rivers of living water."

I n the early 1980s there was a commercial for Memorex cassette tapes. It showed a beautiful wine glass and was accompanied by the sound of a woman with a strong operatic voice singing—and the glass shattered. The words "Is it live or is it Memorex?" would appear on the screen and the camera would pan from the glass shards to the tape player. I suggest that our faith can also be described as authentic or artificial, real or fake, live or Memorex.

In John, the Holy Spirit is identified as streams of living water. Why would God describe the Holy Spirit as water, streams of living water? Water is an extraordinary substance, exceptional in nearly all of its physical and chemical properties. In fact, Aristotle, one of the greatest philosophers, taught the doctrine of the four elements: earth, wind, fire, and water. He retained water as a central principle or element of cosmology.

And from then until now, the behavior of water cannot be totally understood. It covers three-fourths of the earth's surface and has a tremendous impact on our plant life. It helps shape the continents. It moderates our weather and allows organisms to survive. Life on planet Earth would be impossible without water. All life forms rely on water, from simple bacteria to complex multicellular plants and animals. Human beings are composed of approximately 70 percent water. Everything that is alive on this planet depends on water to exist.

Likewise, we depend on the move of the Holy Spirit. This is not an environmental science lesson; this is a Holy Ghost lesson. Fresh water is one of our most important natural resources. We need it to live, and there is no substitute for it. Likewise, the Holy Spirit is the most important spiritual resource. We need the spirit to live, and there is no substitute for the Spirit of God moving in the people of God.

Just as water is necessary for growth and cleansing, the Holy Spirit is necessary for growth and cleansing, and we need it to move us into our destiny. Just as we need water to live, we need the Holy Spirit to live. That is why, as we look at the text, Jesus proclaims on that great day, "If any man or woman thirsts, let him or her come to me and drink." But too often when we are thirsty, we go to the wrong fountain to quench our thirst, not realizing that what we consume in our atmosphere, our thoughts, our conversations, comes out to us in the broken and empty times of life.

So many people throw in the towel during the broken and empty times of life. We allow depression, guilt, shame, rejection, downsizing, and sickness to steal our joy, kill our hopes and dreams. We commit spiritual suicide as a people and sometimes as a church. But I know that you can have confidence in the midst of a storm. You can determine in your innermost being that God is more than enough. You can say and sing, "I've got faith," but when divine consideration calls your name like it did Job, then you discover if you are a yielded vessel. Then and only then will the Holy Spirit burst forth streams of strength to give you the power to push through those broken and empty times of life so that you can testify, "All of my help comes from the Lord." When you come to those seasons as the hymn writer so nobly puts it, "In seasons of distress and grief, my soul has often found relief." We need an anchor. We need a fresh anointing, we need a fresh spirit, and the text gives us some thoughts on this matter.

First of all, the Holy Spirit restores your strength and revives your mind during the rough times of life. Jesus was faced with great opposition. He was rejected by people who had been praying and waiting on him to come. They saw his miracles and still mistreated him. His brothers taunted him in John 7:4. They said to him, "Show yourself to the world." Don't let people provoke you because they can't see what God is doing. Don't get caught up trying to prove things to them and get tricked into moving before

God's timing says so. Let the Holy Spirit revive your mind. The spirit will give you the wisdom to be still and know. In ancient Jewish tradition, water is symbolic of wisdom. The Holy Spirit gives wisdom to those who trust in the Lord.

Don't worry about what people think about you or what they say about you. God has the last word. God says, "Fear not, for I have redeemed you, I have called you by your name, you are mine." The word says, "No weapon formed against you shall prosper" (Isaiah 54:17). God has the last word. Don't give people the power to determine your destiny. Don't give them the power to determine your response or determine your significance. Don't let pressure, people, problems, panic, or impatience make you do anything before your appointed time. The Holy Spirit will revive your mind to the things of God, the touch of God, and the timing of God, so you can push through persistent trouble.

Second, the Holy Spirit will also refresh your outlook during the dry seasons of life. I know it might sound strange to put "refresh" and "dry" in the same sentence. But when you're on an assignment for God, when you've walked with God for a little while, you learn how God does things. The way up is down; you must be abased before grace can abound. David had to walk through the valley before the table could be prepared in the presence of his enemies.

It wasn't Jesus's time for public show but personal ministry. It was his season of preparation for his pubic promotion. The Holy Spirit will refresh your outlook on your assignment during those dry seasons. John 7:10 says, "But after his brothers had gone to the festival, then he also went, not publicly but as it were in secret."

Many readers became confused by the fact that Jesus said, "My time has not yet come," and then immediately after his brothers left, he went. What we need to recognize is that there are two levels of thinking going on here. His brothers were thinking tabernacle timing. Jesus was thinking Passover timing. He was preparing for his finale. Jesus's brothers tried to wear him down and make him move before his time. We have all had people press us and manipulate us to do things their way. "If he were my husband ... If she was my child ... If I were in charge ..."

Manipulation is witchcraft. The Greek word for witchcraft is *python*. A python is a snake, a boa constrictor. It squeezes the life out of its prey. It squeezes the breath out of its victim. Breath represents the Spirit, and only the Sprit can give life. Thus, people with python spirits—rebellious, unteachable, and manipulative—seek to squeeze the life, the breath, the Spirit out of you and the church. Jesus's brothers were trying to squeeze the life, the Spirit, the anointing out of him. The Holy Spirit will refresh your outlook, revive your mind, and restore your strength to be obedient to God that his plans might come to pass in your life. God will give you the strength to stand in the presence of your enemies.

Finally, the Holy Spirit will Resurrect the dead seasons in your life. Just before John 7, Jesus was deserted by disciples who had been walking with him. His blood brothers then ridiculed him, and the religious leaders were looking to discredit him and take his life. Jesus was in a dead season and dry place.

Although he spoke the word of God, the people were dead to the things of God. It was a dry place and dead place because some of them even knew that the religious leaders sought to destroy Jesus and they did nothing. In verse 25 some of the people of Jerusalem began to ask, "Is not this man whom they are trying to kill?" It was a dry place, a dead place because the sin of silence and omission was present among the people even when they came to worship. It was their commemoration of God's goodness to them during their Exodus from Egypt and the completion of the harvest season. It was the most popular festival, called by some the Feast of the Lord. But it was the place where they sought to discredit the Lord. It was a reminder of their freedom from the house of bondage in Egypt and was supposed to keep the Israelites from pride and conceit.

So they came, they gathered and celebrated, but it was still a dry and dead place. It was the last day of the celebration, and on the last day, Jesus stood up and in a loud voice declared, "Let anyone who is thirsty come to me, and let the one who believes in me drink. As the scripture has said, Out of the believers heart shall flow rivers of living water." On the last day of the Feast of Tabernacles, they drew water out of the pool of Siloam, the only freshwater spring in the area. Its name means "sent." It was symbolic of the pouring out of the power, the pouring of the Spirit of God on their lives. It was here that Jesus made a bold declaration: "Let anyone who is thirsty come to me, and let the one who believes in me drink." Jesus was making a connection between himself, who was sent, and the pool of Siloam, which means "sent." The water represented the Spirit of God during the festival. It represented the power of God in their lives to protect, provide, progress, and preserve. It represented the blessings of God in their lives.

You see, John knew that there was more to the Spirit than salvation. He knew that the spirit gives us the Power for God- sized things to happen in our lives. That's why Memorex just won't do. We need the power of the Holy Spirit to restore, revive, refresh, and resurrect some things in our lives today. Today Jesus wants to put the power of his spirit in us so that his power might come out of us. And when we put it in us, healing will be manifested. When we put it in us, we get deliverance from our enemies. When it's in us, there will be a peace that surpasses all understanding. When it's in us, there will be a day of Pentecost in this church like never before.

We need the Spirit so we can witness with power. We need to be baptized with water, and we need to be filled with the Holy Spirit so we can win new souls to Jesus Christ.

THE PROMISED HELPER

———— ∝ ————

John 14:15–16 (NKJV)

*"If you love me, keep my commandments. And I
will pray the Father, and he will give you another
helper, that he may abide with you forever."*

I n 1778 the British were feasting in Philadelphia while
the American revolutionaries were freezing in Valley
Forge. The event that turned the tide occurred on the
other side of the Atlantic in Paris, on February 6, 1778,
when Silas Dean and his team of negotiators worked out
a treaty of alliance between the United States and France.
Communication being as it was, they didn't have a fax. So
it took three months for the document to cross the ocean. It
arrived in York, PA, on May 2, 1778, where it was placed in
the hands of the Continental Congress, who approved it on
May 4, and one day later it reached General Washington.
Recognizing the importance of the alliance, Washington
declared May 6 a day of celebration. In those days of

history, it ranked right up there with July 4. Read part of Washington's proclamation:

> It having pleased the Almighty ruler of the
> Universe propitiously to defend the cause
> of the U.S.A. and finally by raising us
> up a powerful friend, among the Princes
> of the Earth, to establish our liberty and
> independence upon lasting foundations;
> it becomes us to set apart a day, for fully
> acknowledging the divine goodness, and
> celebrating the important event which we
> owe to this benign interposition. Were it
> not for the assistance of a powerful friend,
> the American cause might easily have
> been lost, we would be singing, God save
> the Queen.

With this image in mind, let's return to the Upper Room in the city of Jerusalem, where Jesus's disciples gathered to celebrate the Passover. The writer of the fourth gospel sets the scene in somber shades of pathos and human emotion. He tells us that Jesus knew it was his time to leave, and "having loved his own who were in the world, he loved them to the end." The narrative is surrounded by defeat, the darkness of despair, the shattering pain of separation and death. But in that darkness Jesus's face shines with light, glowing like the central figure in a masterpiece painting: "I will ask the Father, and he will give you another helper, to be with you forever. I will not leave you orphaned ... but the helper (advocate) the Holy Spirit whom the Father will send in my name."

Translators have struggled to find an appropriate word to capture the meaning of the Greek word *Paraclete*. When one examines the word *paracletos* in detail, we catch something of the riches of the doctrine of the Holy Spirit. It really means "someone is called in." The King James Version renders it "comforter"—unfortunate word, for it tends to limit the spirit's work to comfort and consolation in times of trouble. Others have used "advocate"—called in to plead the cause of someone under a charge. But when we get down to where we really live, it's hard to beat the identification of the Holy Spirit as "the Helper." Jesus promises a helper, a powerful friend, who is none other than the spirit of God.

The same spirit who brooded over the chaos of nothingness and brought forth creation, the same spirit who led the people out of Egyptian bondage, the same spirit who healed the sick and liberated the oppressed through the ministry of Jesus, the same spirit who strengthened Jesus in Gethsemane, the same spirit who raised Jesus from the dead, the same spirit who invaded the lives of the first disciples on Pentecost; the living, loving, life-giving spirit of God that we saw in Jesus is now our helper, our powerful friend.

In the hour of darkness, under the shadow of death, when it feels for all the world as if we are going down for the last time, isn't it good to know that we are not alone, that we have been given the helper to lead us into all truth, to guide our thoughts daily, to keep us from stumbling?

There are some doom-and-gloom Christians who are constantly warning us that the end is near. Listen to them, and you will get the idea that the world has fallen so far, things have become so bad. This is the religion of the hopeless, of those who feel that there is nothing they can do to prepare for the worst. But that is not the way Jesus tells his disciples to live. When they asked the question, "What shall we have?" Jesus said, "I will be with you!" Jesus met his disciples in their fears, doubts, frustrations, and dilemmas. We must also remember that God does not forget his children who are victims of fear, doubt, and frustrations. He gives us the interior resources to bear the burdens and tribulations of life. When the lamp of hope flickers and the candle of faith runs low, he restoreth our souls, giving us renewed strength to carry on.

Try to put yourself in the place of the first readers of this gospel. Try to imagine how it felt to live under the oppressive hell of Roman occupation, with all the power of the emperor stacked against you, the hungry lions growling for their dinner in the arena. Imagine how it felt to be politically and economically powerless, shut out because you refused to say "Caesar is Lord."

Let's bring it down home. Some of you know what it feels like to be economically and politically powerless, having come through the depression. Some of you know how it feels to take a stand for righteousness and be shut down, jailed and beaten because you take a stand for what's right. If you can put yourself in those conditions, you can understand the realism of Jesus's words: "If the world hates you, be aware that it hated me, before it hated you. If they persecuted me, they will persecute you. "In the world you shall have tribulation: but be of good cheer, I have overcome the world."."

There's no denying the tough realities of human experience, no avoiding the pain of suffering, no hiding from the persecution. But in the crucibles of suffering, we hear the sound of laughter, the song of gladness, the voice of hope, because we know that Christ has overcome the power of evil and is present with us through the Holy Spirit. The Helper comes to empower us to live victoriously in this world not to help us pack our bags for the next world. The Holy Spirit is Christ present among us, saying, "You will have pain, but our pain will turn into joy. ... I will see you again, and your hearts will rejoice and no one will take your joy from you. Be of good cheer; I have overcome the world."

In his letter to the church at Corinth, Paul describes the way we experience the help of God:

> Let us give thanks to the God and Father of our Lord Jesus Christ ... the God from whom all help comes! He helps us in all our troubles, so that we are able to help others who have all kind of troubles, using the same help that we have received from God. Just as we have a share in Christ's many sufferings, so also through Christ we share in God's great help. We know that just as you share in our sufferings, you also share in the help we receive (II Cor 1:3–7, Good News Bible).

Paul describes a marvelous chain reaction in which we receive God's help in our troubles and we are enabled to help others with the same kind of help we receive. But this help comes only to those who share in the sufferings of others. The miracle of grace is that the helper helps us in our own troubles when we help others in theirs.

In the summer of 1990 a group of American clergypersons shared in a mission to Johannesburg, South Africa. They worked and visited with men and women whose faith had been forged in the furnace of apartheid, ridicule, and persecution because of the prophetic stand for justice, equality, and nonviolence. They were black Christians who have suffered the violence of racism and white Christians who have entered the sufferings of black people around them. But the reality of it all is they faced very difficult times.

When you visit with people like these you find yourself asking, "Why are they smiling? Where do they find such joy?" Their joy comes from the same places as their pain; it comes from knowing that suffering can result in a new life. Their laughter emerges from the same place as their tears. Their gladness is found only through sorrow. Jesus said, the kind of gladness a woman feels when she experiences the very real pain of child birth, comes in knowing that we have a powerful friend. And their hope comes from knowing that the helper has come.

The high moments of our lives need to be remembered, and often we need something to force us to remember. At the first Jordan, Joshua led the people to build a monument from twelve stones taken from the Jordan. It was to be a reminder of God's hand leading them after the battle with the Philistines. Samuel set up a stone and called it Ebenezer, "Hitherto the Lord has helped us."

The Holy Spirit brings the assurance that God is with us, even when the way is dark.

Prayer, the Gateway to Spiritual Power

——— ✗ ———

John 14:13, 14 (NLT)

"You can ask for anything in my name, and I will do it, so that the Son can bring glory to the Father. Yes, ask me for anything in my name, and I will do it."

Spiritual empowerment is made possible through prayer. God sends his Holy Spirit upon us in answer to prayer. The first requirement of the evangelist is to pray in the name of Jesus. Praying in the name of Jesus is praying in the spirit of Christ. It is the Holy Spirit who lifts the soul into the Holy of Holies. It is the Holy Spirit who actually does the praying for you. It is he who assures us that God is completely adequate for all our needs. How does one know this? It is God's mind in you knowing in and through you. The power to witness is not your power. It is really the great cosmic power flowing through you. This power is not something that you are able to create in yourself. It is the gift of God through the Holy Spirit. If you are to receive this power from your Holy Spirit, you must surrender yourself entirely to him in prayer. "You can ask for anything in my name, and I will do it, so that the Son can bring glory to the Father. Yes, ask me for anything in my name, and I will do it."

The only way to receive spiritual power is to meet the spiritual conditions. You cannot meet these conditions in your own strength. Only the Holy Spirit working in you can give you the power. The Holy Spirit comes in answer to prayer. What is prayer? Prayer is practicing the presence of God. Prayer is becoming aware of God's presence. It is rising beyond the creature to fellowship with the creator. Prayer is communion with God. God is everywhere. The whole universe is filled with the presence of God.

It is listening to the voice of God. It is seeking to know the mind of God. It is striving to do the will of God. It is praise and thanksgiving. It is confession and intercession. It is adoration and glorification of the divine. When we truly pray, God is always there. God always answers the prayers of those who believe. The "prayers of the righteous availeth much." There are times when we refuse to accept God's answers. There are times when we do not understand God's answers. God is free to give the answer, and when God answers prayer, he always does what is best for us. How do you know that God answers prayer? Because the Bible declares it: "You can ask for anything in my name, and I will do it, so that the Son can bring glory to the Father. Yes, ask me for anything in my name, and I will do it." God has promised to answer prayers. When we pray in faith, God answers. Sometimes the answer is "Yes!"; sometimes the answer is "No!"; and sometimes the answer is "Not yet!"

What to do when God says yes:

The hymn writer James Montgomery wrote: **"Prayer is the soul's sincere desire, Un-uttered or expressed; the motion of a hidden fire that trembles in the breast."** Prayer at its best is reaching out in an effort to contact God. God is eternally available, for God is everywhere. Prayer at its best is listening to God. When a person truly prays, God is recognized as the initiator. It is God who is reaching down to us. He is speaking to us. Our task is to pay attention. True prayers are therefore responding to the divine initiative. It is waiting on God. It is responding to God. It is saying yes to God. It is surrendering to God. Charles Wesley wrote these words: "O God, visit then this soul of mine; pierce the gloom of sin and grief; Fill radiantly divine, Scatter all my unbelief, more and more display thyself, shining to the perfect day."

If you want God to say yes to you, you must first say yes to him. If you want to hear God's yes, you must make his will your will. You must submit your purpose to the plan of God. You must transform your desire to conform to the nature of God. You must be able to pray, "Thy will be done on earth, as it is in heaven." When this is done, you can be assured that God's answer to your prayer will be yes. When God says yes, nobody can say no. Not the devil nor hell nor any other creature can overrule God's will. God's yes is final, complete, and eternal. God has more ways to say yes than earth and hell can say no. The forces of evil may say no, but God's yes will prevail. God say yes to Moses; Pharaoh said no, but God's yes overruled Pharaoh's no. The children of Israel left for the Promised Land and Pharaoh could not stop them. When God says yes, we must believe him, obey him, and give him the praise. You may not understand how God will bring it to pass, but believe him anyway. You may not know how or where he is leading, but trust him, follow him, and he will give you the victory.

What to do when God says No:

There are times when God answers our prayers with a resounding no. When Jesus prayed in the Garden of Gethsemane, he said, "My Father, if this cup cannot be taken away unless I drink it, your will be done." It was in the Garden of Gethsemane during the darkest hour that Jesus prayed and God said no to his only Son. There are times when God says no to us. It is during such times we must not rebel. We must say, like Christ, "Nevertheless, not my will but thine be done."

A story is told of a little girl who was looking forward so much to her Sunday school picnic, and she prayed that God would give them a good day. In her home there lived an uncle who did not believe in God, and he ridiculed the young girl's prayer. He said, "God isn't interested in you. He's not interested in your Sunday school picnic. He's not concerned with giving you a good day." But the young girl kept on praying that God would give them a good day for their Sunday school picnic. Well, believe it or not, when the time came for the picnic, it was raining—it was a dreadful day. Of course, the uncle took advantage of this and said, "There, I told you so. God didn't hear your prayers; God didn't answer your prayer." But the little girl was not outdone. Very lovingly and with a smile on her face, she said, "Oh yes, Uncle, God has answered my prayer—He has simply said no."

Sometimes we who are fathers say no to our children, and surely it is right and fitting that our heavenly father, at least from time to time, answer our prayers by saying no. God hears and God answers prayer—not in our time, and sometimes he answers by saying no. I contend that even when he says no, even when it appears as if he has not answered our prayer, blessings come through the apparent unanswered prayer.

Paul had a prayer that was asking something specific of God: "And lest I should be exalted above measure by the abundance of the revelations, a thorn in the flesh was given to me, a messenger of Satan to buffet me, lest I be exalted above measure." We don't know what Paul's thorn was. Some say it was a form of epilepsy, some say it was an eye disease. I don't think it really matters. He had a thorn that brought him suffering and he prayed three times: "I pleaded with the Lord three times that it might depart from me. What did God say? And he said unto me, **'My Grace is sufficient for you; for my strength is made perfect in weakness.'"**

God said no to Paul's prayer, but at the same time he said, "My strength is made perfect in your weakness. I'm going to make you strong; I'm going to use you for my glory.

I'm going to help you to maturity." When God says no, we must have faith to say: "Have thine own way, have thine own way; Thou art the potter, I am the clay. Mold me and make me after thy will, while I am waiting, yielded and still."

Finally, what to do when God says Not Yet:

God does not always answer our prayers when we want him to. Our time is not always the right time. When we pray God often answers our prayers by saying "Not yet." Someone has said: "You cannot hurry God." There are times when we pray for the right thing at the wrong time. If God would give it to us when we want it, it might prove to be the very source of destruction. We want it, but God knows that we cannot handle it at this time; therefore, he says "Not yet."

We find Elijah running for his dear life from Jezebel. He ran a whole day and came to a juniper tree and said to God, "I have had enough, Lord. Take my life, for I am no better than my ancestors who have already died." Wouldn't it have been a tragedy if God had answered Elijah's prayer? God didn't answer Elijah's prayer then but simply said "Not yet." Some time later we find Elijah journeying with his servant, Elisha, the one who was to carry on when Elijah would finish his work. It was as these two men of God journeyed and fellowshipped that God prepared the chariot of fire and took his servant Elijah to be with him. What an exodus! What a dramatic conclusion to the life of this mighty man of faith. But what a tragedy it would have been if God had answered Elijah's prayer when he wanted it. God answers every prayer—not our way, not in our time; sometimes he says "Not yet."

You remember the classical story of Augustine—the Black Bishop of Hippo—a saintly man of God, who in his earliest years tasted every sin that could be tasted. Read Augustine's confessions—a classic story of a man finding faith. When Augustine was a young boy, Monica, his mother, prayed for him, but it seemed as if her prayers were going unanswered because Augustine seemed to be getting further and further away from God. When Augustine decided to leave his native shores of North Africa and go to Italy—which at that time was a cesspool of iniquity—Monica, his mother, knelt on the seashore and as the ship was carrying her son across the Mediterranean, she prayed, "O God, stop him from going." But Augustine got to Italy, Augustine got to Rome, and it was in Rome when he was converted to the Christian faith. God didn't answer Monica's prayer when she wanted him to because God answered the prayer when he was ready to use Augustine.

When God says "Not yet," we must have faith enough to wait on God. When David killed Goliath, Israel as a nation was ready to make him king. David might have been ready, but God said "Not yet." For fourteen years David waited on God. In God's own time, he made David king of Israel.

When you pray and God says "Not yet," wait on him! "They that wait upon the Lord, shall renew their strength; they shall mount up with wings as eagles, they shall run and not be weary, they shall walk and not faint." When your answer is delayed, do not despair. God knows that you are not ready to receive the answer. Through his guidance he is getting you ready. The Holy Spirit works through prayer.

Works cited

Montgomery, James. "Prayer Is the Soul's Sincere Desire." (A.M.E. Zion Bicentennial Hymnal # 450).October, 1996. Charlotte, NC

Pollard, Adelaide A. "Have Thine Own Way, Lord." (A.M.E. Zion Bicentennial Hymnal # 492). October, 1996. Charlotte, NC

SERMONS ON THE
HOLY COMMUNION

———— ⤫ ————

T he Lord's Supper, although a memorial of a death, is not a funeral, as if Jesus were still dead. Rather, we observe this memorial knowing that death held Jesus only three days—and knowing that death will not hold us forever, either. We rejoice that Jesus conquered death and has set free all who were enslaved by a fear of death. Coming to the Lord's table and having communion should be a celebration, not a funeral.

Every time we participate, we should be mindful of the great meaning involved in this ceremony. When we examine ourselves, we often find sin. This is normal; it is not a reason to avoid the Lord's Supper. It is a reminder that we need Jesus in our lives.

As we examine ourselves, we need to look around to see whether we are treating one another in the way that Jesus commanded. If you are united with Christ and I am united to Christ, then we are united to each other. By participating together in the Lord's Supper, we picture the fact that we are one body in Christ, one with each other, with responsibilities toward one another.

The Lord's Supper is rich in meaning. That is why it has been a prominent part of the Christian tradition throughout the centuries. Sometimes it has been allowed to become a lifeless ritual, done more out of habit than with meaning. When a ritual loses meaning, some people overreact by stopping the ritual altogether. The better response is to restore the meaning.

Prayerfully, these messages will be helpful for us to renew the meaning of our custom.

You Can Always Eat
at the King's Table

———————— ∝ ————————

2 Samuel 9:13(NIV)

**"And Mephibosheth lived in Jerusalem,
because he always ate at the king's table,
and he was crippled in both feet."**

C ome and go with me to Jerusalem, the seat of political power where King David reigns. He has had a full life. You remember that as a shepherd boy he slew the Philistine giant Goliath and became a celebrated hero of all of Israel. The women would sing and dance, saying, "Saul has killed his thousands, and David has slain ten thousand." David eventually had to flee from King Saul's jealous, murderous wrath, but his life was saved because of his friendship with Jonathan, Saul's son. Now, years later, a prosperous, older, and wiser David returns to Saul's old mansion and asks, "Is there yet any of the house of Saul, that I may show the kindness of God unto him?" The houseman, Ziba, replies, "There is still a son of your best friend

Jonathan, Mephibosheth; he is crippled in both feet and living in Lobedar."

Now Lo-debar was a rural county of Jerusalem. It was the "low end." No one really thrived in Lo-debar. Its inhabitants were probably known in Jerusalem as "families at risk." Children living in families with four or more of the following characteristics are considered at high risk. You know what a high-risk home is? A home where there are not two loving, healthy parents; where the family income is below the poverty line; a place where the head of the household is a high school dropout; where the parents do not have steady or fulltime employment; a place where the family is receiving welfare benefits; and there is no adequate healthcare available. The Lodebarian's Defense fund, that age-old child-advocacy organization, probably reported in their version of the kids count fact book that in Lo-debar last year, 78 children were victims of child abuse, there were 786 families at risk, 193 teenagers became parents, 1,050 juveniles were arrested, and 360 babies were born weighing less than 5 pounds because their mothers were teenagers with little or no parental care. I don't know if those are exact Lo-debar statistics, but based on some of the places we know here in America, we can relate to Lo-debar.

People in Lo-debar are the working poor. Their jobs do not pay enough for them to reach the poverty level. Mothers in Lo-debar cannot find affordable childcare. Fathers in Lobedar have to work double shifts just to make ends meet. Mephibosheth, the grandson of King Saul and the son of Prince Jonathan, is living in Lobedar.

Ziba informs us that Mephibosheth was crippled in both feet. I'm sure Mephibosheth, being crippled, received enough Social Security supplemental income benefits to survive in Lo-debar but never enough money to get out of Lo-debar. This text teaches us that it's possible to be broken and yet whole, to be battered and yet be blessed, to be stigmatized and yet be magnified. Because life is never absolute, one can be weak and yet strong; one can be burdened and yet blessed; one can be down and yet up; one can be a beggar and yet also a benefactor. And because life is relative and it has it ups and downs, its weaknesses and its strengths, its brokenness and its flaccidity, peace comes when you can "eat continually at the king's table, though you are lame in both feet."

You see, the word "handicapped" describes one's inability and the word "crippled" describes one's physiology; but the word "lame" describes one's social condition in the midst of his spiritual depravity. Not only is he down and out, but he is so far down and out he can hear nobody pray. So in that case, man is lame—not in his toe, not in his ankle, not in one foot, but he has a double dose of predestined inferiority and is relegated to the "outdoor committee." "He did eat continually at the king's table, though he was lame in both feet."

Mephibosheth was only five years old when Jonathan, his father, and King Saul, his grandfather, both fell in the same battle on Mount Gilboa and his family fled in fear for safety. In a rush to get out of town, the nursemaid picked up this young child who had just learned to run and enjoy the flowers and the sunshine and to know that his legs caused him to be something of a marvelous creation of God, and at the tender age of five years old the nursemaid dropped him. His ankles were crushed. And now the one who was born to walk could walk no longer. The man-child who was created to be proud as a king found himself wallowing in the dust. He who was to inherit the banquet table found himself in the street as a beggar. His original name Merib-Baal, which means "he who opposes Baal," was changed that day by his mother to the name Mephibosheth, which means "he who multiplies us." From that day on, every time someone called his name, it reminded him that he had fallen. Every time his mother called him by his new name, he was reminded that somehow he had become something other than what he was supposed to be. His name became a stigma, a con-demnation, a reminder that not only had he been broken, the evidence of his life was that by being broken he was separated from God. And yet in his brokenness, in his fallen-ness, in his separation, the scripture says, he did eat at the king's table, though he was lame in both feet.

The writers had to tell the story because every time they spoke of Mephibosheth, they were talking about you and me. They wanted us to know that there is a little Mephibosheth in every one of us and we "ain't all that." What we have on us does not define what we have in us. Today, we may look as though "we've got it all together," but before the King we are broken. There has been a fall in your life, and because you have fallen, you have been separated. Your new name has become your stigma. We can't call you a saint anymore; we have to call you a sinner because you fell—you'll never be whole again. You will never be worthy to come to the banquet on your own. No one is broken by the statute of law; anyone who is lame would never appear before the king. You had to be whole; you had to be together. All parts of your body had to be functioning; the king must never be reminded of anything that was imperfect, and so the law was that at the king's table no one could come but those who were whole. It is from the law. Love stepped in.

Jesus, in spite of our brokenness, said, "I will bless you anyhow." In spite of what we are, the King said, "I remember what you were supposed to be; I remember that you are a child of the King. Though your sins separate you from me, you may come to the table. You can kneel at the table. You can cry at the table. You can receive bread and wine at the table. You can find relief at the table. You may remain at the table until something strange starts happening deep down within your soul, though you have no right to be here. I am the King and this is my table, and I will do what I will do and I will invite whomever I choose. Whosoever will, let him come. You do not have to be whole; you just have to be seeking holiness. You do not have to be perfect; you just have to be prayerful. You do not have to be right; you just have to be thirsting for righteousness. You do not ever have to have joy in you life, but if you come, I will give you what you need. Come on to the table and eat continually. I am so glad that I have a God who never runs out of his supply. He has what I need, when I need it, how I need it, as I want it, in a way that I will be blessed. He feeds me today, and in the storehouse he has something for me tomorrow. His storehouse never runs out. Every day he gives me what I need. The scriptures tell me that I can eat continually. Let me tell you why we come to the table.

First, we come to the table because there is joy at the table.

You may not feel good on the outside, but something makes you feel good on the inside. The world is disturbing you and turning you upside down. But there is something on the inside that turns you right side up. It is unmerited favor; it is a divine anointing, an imputation of the Holy Spirit that gives you a peace and release that you never had before. If you do not know why you feel like you do, but you know what you know and there is joy in your life.

Men want you to cry, but you cannot help but smile. Men want you to talk about your burdens, but you tell them he is blessing you. There is joy at the table. That is why we come to the table. Men can take your health and give you weakness and give you disease, but God has something to give you that men cannot give and the world cannot take away. There is joy at the table.

Second, we come to the table because there is fellowship at the table.

It is one thing to be broken and to be alone. However, one will always discover spiritual strength in heart because he knows there is someone who shares in his brokenness is at the table. As the Holy Ghost is blessing you, he also shares his strength with all who are at the table. Though you are alone, you are not lonely. Though you must walk your own path, you know you never walk alone because there is fellowship at the table. Often in the midnight hour, when your burdens are heavy, something within your soul causes you to begin singing C.A. Tindley's hymn: "Courage my Soul, and let us journey on, though the night be dark it won't be very long. But, Thanks be to God the morning light appears andThe storm is passing over, Hallelujah."

Finally, we come to the table because every now and then, we know we are going to meet the king at the table.

Every time Mephibosheth came into the banquet room, there sat at the head of the table an empty chair. The chair had the insignia in the honor of the king a star with twelve angels to the five points of the star. The star was the Star of David. This empty chair was especially reserved for the king. Although many times the banquet room was full, the empty chair was always the central focus. Unannounced and often without warning, the king would appear, and those who fellowshipped there, those who found joy there, those who feasted there knew that the king would come and appear at the table. Oh what a joy to see the king at the table, to see his face, to know of his mercy, to know that he loved me in spite of what I am. To know that he makes a way out of no way for me and to know that every day that I could come and dine here because this table belongs to the king.

I am not worthy to come to this place. I am broken, battered, and bruised, but thank God, I can come to the table for I know every now and then the king will show up at the table, and when he comes, there is joy; when he comes, there is peace; when he comes, there is mercy; when he comes, there is love.

Thank God for the King's table.

A Meal You Cannot Afford to Miss

———— ⊂✕⊃ ————

Luke 24:30–32 (25–35) NRSV

"When he was at the table with them, he took bread, blessed it and broke it, and gave it to them. Then their eyes were opened, and they recognized him; and he vanished from their sight. They said to each other, Were not our hearts burning within us while he was talking to us on the road, while he was opening the scriptures to us?"

Ever been on your way somewhere to do something routine and had the extraordinary happen? That was the experience of a group in our text. In this text, we find the word had already reached almost every hamlet and corner of Jerusalem that Jesus, who had faced excruciating suffering on Friday, was now missing from the tomb. In the midst of this news, there were those who unequivocally proclaimed that Jesus had done just what he said he would do. However, there were those who circulated rumors that it was not the power of God that had resurrected Jesus but some of his disciples who had stolen his body, a lie that attempted to diminish any authority given to the power of the resurrection rumor.

While there were those who believed and those who sought to deceive, there were also those who wouldn't confess it until they actually saw Jesus for themselves. I mean, there were those who believed he had the power to get up, but they wouldn't confess it until they actually saw the physical scars, bruises, and abrasions that he had suffered on Friday to validate his resurrection on Sunday.

So in Luke 24, we find two disciples walking down the Emmaus road. Emmaus was six miles south of Jerusalem. They got out of Jerusalem to go to Emmaus to escape the embarrassment and shame of believing in a savior who had failed to save himself. Now they were walking down this Emmaus road with their heads hung low, hurt in their hearts and pain in their spirits, but it was in the midst of their hurt, disappointment, and embarrassment that Jesus showed up by the wayside.

So Jesus saw these disciples walking and brief conversation ensued, and Jesus ended up at their house, breaking bread, blessing it, and having supper. According to the biblical record, this was the first supper that Jesus had after the resurrection. So in Luke 24, we find Jesus having supper after the resurrection. It is the resurrection that establishes a new timeline that contains an expectancy and punctuates that some things have changed. The resurrection is about the old being eradicated and a new being validated.

It is about the new forward march to the future. Even in the Roman calendar, time moves from BC to AD because of the resurrection. That's why you have a resurrection in your own life, where you confess with your mouth the Lord and Savior Jesus Christ, and believe in your hear that God raised him from the dead; then you are given the right and the authority to confess boldly that old things are passed away and behold all things have become new.

Isn't it good to know that we can come to this supper today, on World Communion Sunday, to share in a meal that takes us to a new level in our relationship with God? When you leave this meal today, folks might want to remember you for what you used to do, and where you used to go, and who you used to be, but look where you are now. After today, yesterday was your past; today you are walking into your future. This meal sets you apart from your past, so you cannot afford to miss this meal. It's important to be at this meal **TO GET YOUR ASSIGNMENT.**

Jesus decided to have this supper with two disciples who had their heads hung low and pain in their hearts because they didn't have proof of his resurrection. But the food was not the main thing on Jesus's mind at this supper. Jesus was not at this supper because he didn't have anywhere to eat. He was there because he understood that even after the resurrection he had an assignment to fulfill as a resurrected savior. There were some who needed direction, inspiration, and information. And if there is anything for us to learn from this, we must learn that all of us have an assignment to fulfill. That's what P. T. Forsyth was talking about when he said that Christianity is perfect, not in the sense of being finished, rounded, or symmetrical, but it upholds a perfect ideal that everyone is called to fulfill a noble task before God.

And if you're going to be effective in the twenty-first century with whatever ministry God has given you, it is important for you to know how to discern your assignment. Too many times the church is ill-equipped and potential goes unfulfilled because too many people in the church are simply missing their assignments. Everybody is not called to preach; everybody is not called to teach; everybody is not called to prophesy. We miss our assignment because we think that the assignment must always be at a lofty level. But in truth, your assignment begins when you detect a need in your family, church, or community; in the company where you work, the school you attend, or a relationship you are in. Don't be distracted by the so-called grander things of life and overlook other areas of need that God may have appointed as your assignment.

We need more "I'll go" disciples. Big assignments, "I'll go." Small assignments, "I'll go." Nobody-else-wants-it assignments, "Send me. I'll go." Maybe your assignment is being on a job that you don't really like. But there are times when God will place us in jobs, not just to do the job but to reach some people around us and help us grow up. You could be on an assignment. I know there are some ungodly people with no sense of purpose and no sense of the will of God for their lives. You often wonder why God ever gave you a call to deal with these people, but know that the assignment is not just about you. It's about God!

Whether your assignment is something others are already doing or something of unique design, it is your assignment. It is the need you have been called by God to fill. It is time for you to possess and take proper ownership of the vocation and call that God has deposited in your spirit. There is always a senior citizen who needs a ride somewhere. There is always a child who needs a mentor to guide, motivate, and challenge them for success. There is always room for another choir member, usher, van driver, or nursery worker. Kingdom assignments are not lofty heights; your seat at the table is right where you are!

I am reminded of that poem that Douglas Malloch that says, "If you can't be a pine on the top of the hill, Be a scrub in the valley, but be the best little scrub by the side of the hill; Be a bush if you can't be a tree." "If you can't be a highway, then just be a trail, If you can't be the sun be a star; it isn't by size that you win or fail, be the best of whatever you are."

Second, it's important that you be at this meal to receive soul food..

Not only was Jesus on an assignment at this supper, but consider for a moment that the supper was soul food. What the disciples had at the table with Jesus was not food from the supermarket...... but it was soul food. What they had ministered to their souls. This was not the first time Jesus had broken bread with the disciples and blessed it. In the upper room at the last supper before his resurrection, he took bread, broke it, and blessed it. At the last supper he broke the bread to show what was about to happen to him, but here at this supper, he was breaking bread to show what was about to happen to them.

What Jesus was essentially trying to show the disciples was that once your eyes are open and you begin to proclaim that you know the father because you know Jesus, then persecution will break out. In other words, after the disciples confessed him, Jesus wanted them to know that they would be unpopular among a lot of folk. They were setting themselves up to be dehumanized, rejected, and disrespected. Facing all of this, they needed some soul food. They needed to be fortified—and so do we for the same reasons. The disciples had Jesus in the flesh as their soul food. We have the Bible and the Holy Ghost, and we have to lean on both for our fortification. And in times like these, we need fortification, soul food, more than ever. Why? Because the world is broken and out to break us. This presidential administration has ushered in an intense season of hatred and persecution like never before. We are broken as we stand on the precipice of a shift in the Supreme Court of the United States that could reduce if not eliminate most of the strides of the civil rights movement.

However, let us never forget that not only did Jesus break the bread, but he also blessed it. Yes, you might be broken, but the good news says that you are still blessed. As a matter of fact, I have found that some of the best blessings in my life have come after I was broken. And you are blessed because it's in your brokenness that God is refreshing you, strengthening you, redirecting you. That's why you can go through certain situations that are supposed to destroy you, but through it all when God blesses you, instead of being torn up, you come out fixed up, made up, and raised up because God knows how to bless his children.

Finally, it's important to be at this meal because the supper gave them heartburn.

There is something else to be said about this supper, and that is that after Jesus finished feeding their souls, they had heartburn. Now, understand that they didn't get heartburn from consuming physical food. While Jesus ate their food, he also fed them some food. It was manna from on high. The Bible says he opened unto them the scriptures and began to preach unto them the word of God, beginning with Moses and the prophets, all the things concerning himself. They didn't get heartburn from the bread that Jesus broke at the table, but their hearts burned within because they were with the Bread of Life.

When Jesus finished preaching about Jonah, which was a metaphor for his own death, burial, and resurrection. When he told how Jonah ended up in the belly of a whale for three days and three nights, and how it was on the third day that transformation took place for Jonah, it was like the third day transformation taking place in him.

Then I believe Jesus looked at them and said, "I am he that was dead but am alive for evermore." It was when they realized who Jesus was that they declared, "Did not our hearts burn as the man of God spoke to us by the way?"

When I was growing up, there used to be a commercial that promoted a way to handle heartburn. In the commercial the question was raised, "How do you spell relief?" And the response was spelled out R-O-L-A-I-D-S. After Jesus got through with the disciples, I am sure that from then on they spelled relief J-E-S-U-S!

How do you spell relief? Here's what I believe. When you are lonely, relief is spelled J-E-S-U-S. For he said, "I will never leave you or forsake you." When you are tired, spell relief J-E-S-U-S. For he said, "Come unto me, all ye that labor and are heavy laden, and I will give you rest." When you are burdened, spell it J-E-S-U-S. "Take my yoke upon you and learn of me, for my yoke is easy and my burden is light." When you are hungry, you still spell relief J-E-S-U-S. I heard him say, "I am the bread of life, and anyone who eats of this bread shall never get hungry or thirsty."

CHRISTMAS MESSAGES OF LIGHT AND HOPE

——————⟨✕⟩——————

What an exciting time is the Advent season! It's the beginning of another year of walking through the scripture to experience the life of Christ together. And ofcourse it signals the beginning of the Christmas season.

Advent is an annual reminder to be always ready for the coming of Jesus. It is a season of preparation to celebrate the First Advent—or birth—of Jesus, to receive the risen Christ into our hearts as Savior and Lord and to be ready for Christ's second advent—coming—in final victory.

This is what Advent is really about. It's not about lights and carols and buying presents. True, it is about preparing to celebrate ourselves and our world for the Savior's return at the end of days when things in this world will be set right. No one knows when that day will be, but I do know this: the cries of God's children will not forever be unanswered. "Oh, that you would rend the heavens and come down." Our Savior has come down in the manger of Bethlehem, and he is coming again to answer the cries of his children for peace and justice and the end of all suffering and pain.

BEHOLD THAT STAR

—————— ⋈ ——————

Matthew 2:2 (KJV)

*"For we have seen his star in the east
and have come to worship him."*

W e have before us a story of three wise men or
kings journeying to Bethlehem. You will notice
in the passage that no number is given as to
how many men were there. But in art and literature they
are referred to as three. They are named Caspar, Melchior,
and Balthasar. This is the order that you will find them in.
Caspar is always tall, old, and shown bearded. Melchior is
always a young man without a beard. Balthasar is always
black-skinned or very dark, and small in stature. They came
because they too, like the shepherds, had seen a great light.
According to tradition, exactly twelve days after the shepherds had seen the light. Mathew does not say there were
kings but wise men. They were some type of astrologers
who studied the stars of people's lives. They predicted what
events happened in the lives of people. In those days a king

always kept his astrologers close at hand. Astrology played a part in everyday life. If something unusual appeared in the sky, the competent astrologers of every country made their interpretations known, and that was that. The stars have always played a major role in the destinies of men, whether people accept astrology as fact or an untruth.

In the story of Julius Caesar, he ignored the warning to take care of himself on the ides of March and paid for it with his life. Dozens of astrologers knew that President Kennedy was in personal danger around the time of his assassination, yet nothing could be done to prevent it. So as it is, these three men had seen this great star and instantly knew that a king was being born in Bethlehem. The mystery that lies behind this is no one knows what kind of star appeared. It was bright, illuminating, a star that stood out among other stars. It was said to have been a comet. It was the star that later became known as the Bright and Morning Star. The Greek translation says that the star must have been rising. When an astrologer saw a rising star- it was a sign that someone of great importance was about to be born.

So it is to the wise men that we must go and see this great king having been born. I am so happy to know that so many of us have found the bright and morning star. It's all right to hear about him or to read about him through the scripture. But it's something extraordinary to know the Christ child.

The beautiful thing about it is so many people have come to know him for themselves.

The three wise men were wise indeed to want to come see Jesus for themselves. I'm glad history recorded these wise men as going to the Christ child. It was already destined that coming to Christ would be a source of strength to any wayfaring stranger. When you are lost, he will help you find your way. He has led many a thousand. Even though these three men were strangers and were from different countries, it makes no difference who we are, where we live, for "In Christ there is no East or West, in him no North and South, but one great fellowship of love, throughout the whole wide earth."

There is something bright and glorious about any life in relationship with Jesus. Show me a man or woman who has been with the Lord, and I will show you somebody who has the authority of experience. There is something about knowing this savior, this Christ child, the star of Bethlehem, that the more we see of him, the better we like him. You may not be sufficient, and I may not be sufficient for this or that, but God is able. God is so good that he can bring peace out of confusion, joy out of sorrow, spring out of winter, laughing out of weeping, and holiness out of sin.

Another thing about the story is the fact that these three men brought gifts. But it was something about these gifts that made them special. **Gold** was brought to honor his kingship, **Frankincense** to honor his divinity, and **Myrrh** was to honor his humanity, which was destined for death. Myrrh was used at his burial. When Herod saw the gifts he knew the time was near that his kingship would end. So he set out to destroy him. He had no intention of worshipping the Christ child. What led you to Christ? Was it a Bright and Morning Star ? Was it because you heard of him from someone else?

Each one of us were led to Christ in our own ways. Christ has many ways to lead his children.

This is what makes Jesus so special to some of us. Where others only see trash, he sees something in us worth his attention. Sometimes people we call important look at us and never seem to see us, not really. Take for instance Matthew, nobody saw anything good in him. No one saw anything worthwhile in Matthew, but Jesus did. What about you? Has anyone seen any good in us? Not so with Jesus. The Lord looks on each of us that way. He surely saw something in us, and we can witness today that "the Lord saw something in me." He believed that there was something in me that would respond to his invitation.

The story gets better and better throughout the years. Any Christian could tell you where the way led for many. It was a way of fighting, forging ahead, falling, forgiving, forgetting, finding that the way grows brighter every passing day. The wise men were led by a star, and that star led them all the way to Jesus. That star is still leading men and women, boys and girls to Christ. Following the king—that's what it's all about. I am so glad that he came to earth and found me and I decided to follow Jesus all the way. He is a mighty good leader. As G. A. Young once wrote: Sometimes on the mount, where the sun shines so bright, Sometimes in the valley, in darkness of night, God leads his dear children along. **I hope when you find your Christ you will want to go back and tell someone.** Don't keep it to yourself! You must Go into all the world and witness that He's the Son of God. When the wise men came, they went away with new direction and a new outlook. They didn't go back the same old way. They went home another way. When people are out to do you wrong, remember God warns you and sends you a different way. If you come to the Lord weary, worn, and sad, He will send you away feeling good, Joy bells ringing in your heart. He has made me glad!!

A paralyzed man came to Jesus on a stretcher, carried by four of his friends. There were many people in the house until they could not get close to Jesus. They climbed up on the roof, made a hole in the roof, attached ropes to the stretcher, and lowered their friend down into the room where Jesus was eating supper. When Jesus saw their great faith, he said: "Your sins are forgiven, Get up, pick up your stretcher, and walk." The paralyzed man started walking and the people were amazed, He came to the Lord carried by four, but the Lord sent him walking out the door. He came to the Lord one way, but the Lord sent him another way.

The blind man at Jericho could say, "I once was lost, was blind but now I see." A young married couple used to argue all the time. She nagged all the time. One Sunday night she described what happened when they went to a revival: "False pride used to be our reason for trying to make our marriage work." Since all our friend were saying ours was a bad marriage, our false pride said, "We'll fool our friends." But that night at the revival meeting God gave us the Holy Ghost and the Love of Jesus came into our hearts, and for the first time we tried to make our marriage work because we loved each other. We came to the Lord hateful and proud, but the Lord sent us home Holy and in love. We came to the Lord one way, but the Lord sent us home a different way.

I'm reminded of a great classic movie, *The Poseidon Adventure*. It is the story of a ship that was turned upside down by a storm at sea. The movie centered around the surviving passengers searching for a way out of the ship. One of the central characters, the Reverend Scott, found a way to search for an escape from the rising waters within the ship. He climbed up a Christmas tree and tried to get others to follow him up to the next level of the ship. He kept calling them, "Come on up. It's this way." Only a few would go with him. The others were afraid and one shouted back at him, "Why don't you mind your own business?" He was. He was trying to save them.

When I saw that, I could not help but think how Jesus, the one born to be a king, dared to climb the tree in order to save us, and how he calls us back to him: "It's this way."

In all the uncertainties of your own life, take this away from Christmas with you. In the darkness of uncertainty, let the light of wonder shine on you. Let the light of the star shine on you and guide you to a life of joy and wonder.

The stars shine down on the Land
The stars shine down upon the sea
The stars look up to a mighty God
The stars look down on me.
The stars will shine for a million years
For a million years and a day
For God and I will live and love
When the stars have passed away

GOD'S TIMING IS ALWAYS BEST

---◇---

Galatians 4:4 (1–7) (NKJV)

"But when the fullness of time had come, God sent his Son, born of a woman, born under the law."

E xactly one minute has passed. Isn't it amazing? My watch tracks time. It has a second hand that moves every second. Sixty seconds moves the big hand one step forward to mark the passing of a minute. Isn't it absolutely amazing how long one minute of silence seems but how short one minute seems when you are doing something you enjoy? Did you know that there are only sixteen days until Christmas? That means there are approximately 384 hours until we celebrate the birth of Christ. There are presents to purchase and wrap, parties to attend, people to visit, and we don't have much time left. So why did you just waste one precious moment sitting there doing nothing?

As we begin this Advent celebration, I want us to recognize not only the significance of one moment in time but also of the strategic nature of those moments. We would refer to the strategic nature of time as timing. Have you ever stopped to consider how important timing is to everything that exists? Do you plant tomato plants in November? Do you paint the outside of your house in January? Do you go swimming in the pond during February? No? Why not? It's not the right time! There is a right time for such activities. I think we would all agree that December is not the best time to try starting a diet, right?

Think about the importance of timing in sports. If the timing is off, the quarterback won't connect with his receiver for a completion. It doesn't take a minute to throw off the timing in football. If the timing is off, the basketball player will arrive at the spot before the ball or after the ball is already passed. Think about the importance of timing for our daily lives. If you ever missed a flight because you arrived one minute after boarding, you know the importance of timing. You are delayed at work, but because of the delay, you missed a major accident on the interstate. If you are the parent of a preschooler, you know that if you turn your head for one minute, that preschooler can be long gone and into trouble.

Does one minute make a difference? Just ask those who made it out of the Twin Towers minutes before it collapsed. One moment, one sixty-second interval of time, placed in just the right location, can make all the difference in the world. This message this morning is on the Miracle of the Moment. It is so easy to get wrapped up in the activity of the season that we miss the miracle of Christmas. This Christmas season, let's spend some moments reflecting on the significance of Christ's birth.

Galatians 4:4 is an incredible verse. It says, "But when the fullness of time had come, God sent his Son, born of a woman, born under the law." Did you hear that? God's word says, "When the time came, When the fullness of time had come." At just the right time God sent his Son. That represents the miracle of the moment.

First, He came at the right time

There is a Christmas classic movie titled *Miracle on 34th Street*. It's a wonderful, magical tale about an old man named Kris Kringle who believes he is Santa Claus and wants others to believe in him as well. Looking closely at that movie, there are some important parallels that merit some attention. Kris is trying to instruct a department store Santa prior to the big Thanksgiving Day parade. One has to really look at this story or else you will miss the miracle. Was it just by chance or coincidence that Kris Kringle was there at the parade that day? No! That represents the miracle of the moment. At just the right time, Kris Kringle showed up at the parade and rescued not only the parade but the jobs of Ms. Walker and countless others. Ms. Walker failed to recognize the miracle of the moment. She failed to realize the significance of Kris Kringle being the store Santa at the time.

The Bible says, "When the time came to completion, God sent his Son." But the reality is, most people missed the miracle of the moment. Most people did not recognize the significance of Christ's birth at the time. People were much too busy to pay any attention to the young girl giving birth to her first child out in a stable there in Bethlehem. At just the right time in history Jesus was born. The coming of Christ into the world was not a matter of chance or coincidence. His coming was part of God's divine plan established before the foundation of the world.

Historians tell us that the Roman world was in great expectation, waiting for a deliverer, at the time Jesus was born. The old religions were dying. The old philosophies were empty and powerless to change men's lives. Strange new mystery religions were invading the empire. Religious bankruptcy and spiritual hunger were everywhere. God was preparing the world for the arrival of his Son.

Joseph and Mary went to Bethlehem for one reason. All of these people were living under the oppression of Rome. It had been that way for centuries. The surrounding enemies had conquered Israel, then Judah, then came the deportation to Babylon. That was followed by a time of freedom. Soon the Greeks came, followed by the Romans. The people were oppressed. They needed a Savior and they knew it. The irony is, the Savior came, and yet many did not even know it. Perhaps some of us are depressed today by fear, sin, sorrow, failure, or suffering of some kind. Christmas brings to all of us the good news of the Savior's birth. At just the right time, God sent his son!

Second, he provides at the right time.

Many people will be content to go through the motions. They will endure the busy activity of the season without ever experiencing the miracle of Christmas. But some this holiday season need nothing short of a miracle. The good news is that God comes to us at just the right time with just what we need for the moment.

Prepare for his coming. Open your heart and mind to this great truth about Christ being born—God's only Son coming into the world—becoming God with us—getting down to our eye level—taking upon himself the human experience—enduring all our sins, sorrow, hurts, and shame, and even death—and then winning a victory over all of this for us because he is the Savior. Remember all these basic things about his birth, and then open your heart and mind to this Savior being born in you.

God knows exactly what you are going through. He knows exactly what you need. At just the right time he will come to you and provide what you need for the moment. His timing is always perfect. God not only came at just the right time; He continues to come to us at just the right time. Just when we need him the most. He is there! Romans 5:6 says, "For while we were still sinners, at the appointed moment, Christ died for the ungodly." When do you need a miracle? When you have no more options and no more resources, you are in a position to receive a miracle from God. He has promised to come at just the right time and provide just what you need for the moment.

The legendary songwriter and singer Fanny J. Crosby knew something about the "Faith and love that are in Christ Jesus," and she said so in the many poems she wrote that became gospel songs. Through her songs, her name became prominent in the late nineteenth-century urban revivalism. Although blind since she was eight years old, Fanny Crosby grew up equipped with spiritual insight, and she let her life resound as a hallelujah for Jesus. Thank God for her witness the next time you sing "Saved by Grace" or utter the words to "Blessed Assurance" or hum "Savior, More Than Life to Me." Thank God for her witness as you sing the exultant lines of "To God Be the Glory." These songs represent the simplicity and emotional depth of a soul who by our standards was a helpless creature in need of a miracle from God. At just the right time God gave Fanny Crosby just the words to hymns that you and I need right now: "Praise Him." When you are in need of a Savior, Jesus comes at the right moment.

Finally, he says now is the right time.

It seems we are always waiting for just the right time to do something. We are waiting for just the right time to make that commitment of our life to Christ as Savior and Lord. Maybe you are waiting for just the right time to make that commitment to church membership. Maybe you are waiting for just the right time to commit to a closer walk with Christ.

Maybe you've been waiting for just the right time to give up that bad habit. Second Corinthians 6:2 says, "I heard you in an acceptable time, and I helped you in the day of salvation. Look. Now is the acceptable time; now is the day of salvation."

Now is the right time to make that commitment to Christ. Jesus said in Mark 1:15, "The time is fulfilled, and the Kingdom of God has come near. Repent and believe in the good news!" Now is the right time to make that commitment to Christ and receive God's gift of salvation. Now is the time to join the church. Now is the time to recommit to our marriage and family. Now is the time to renew that commitment to walk in close fellowship with Christ. The right time is now to draw close to the Lord!

One moment in time can determine an eternal destiny. Right now is just such a moment. You don't have to live your life separated from God's love and blessing. Today is the right time to receive God's gift of salvation through Jesus Christ. If you have never made a commitment of your life to Jesus Christ receiving him as your Lord and Savior, then I want to invite you to make that commitment today. This moment can change your earthly direction as well as your eternal destiny.

A story is told of a wealthy man who enjoyed taking his son on business trips. Often on these trips, the man would purchase priceless works of art. He filled his home with these paintings. The boy grew to manhood, and when war broke out, he went to serve his country. In just a few months, the man received word his son had died in battle, trying to save the lives of some of his friends. When the next Christmas came, the man found it difficult to get through the season. The suffering he had experienced was too much. But on Christmas morning, a young soldier came to his door and presented him with a portrait of his son. The young soldier was among those whose lives had been saved. The father placed the portrait over his fireplace. He would often sit in front of it and think of his son. Several years later, the man died. His lawyer carried out his will. The instructions were that the home and everything in it were to be sold at auction. The first thing to be sold was the portrait of the man's son. When the auctioneer called out, "What am I bid?" no one seemed to want the portrait. To move things along, a man in the back said, "Ten Dollars." The auctioneer said, "Going, going, gone. Sold for ten dollars. The auction is over." There was an outcry as people shouted, "What! What do you mean?" The auctioneer explained, "The terms of the will are very clear. Whoever chooses the son receives everything."

Choose Jesus and you will have everything! Choose Jesus and you will have abundant life on earth and eternal life with Christ in heaven. If you will choose the Son, you will have it all, for you will have the light of life.

WHEN GOD MESSES WITH YOUR PLANS

---◇---

Matthew 1:18–25

Brothers! Can you remember those days of your engagement? You had fallen in love with the dream of your life. And what made it even better: She had fallen in love with you too! There came that time when you made up your mind to ask her to marry you. And she agreed! This morning, I want to speak about the marriage of Joseph and Mary.

When God messes with your plans! Engagements were handled differently in those days than they are now. Marriages were prearranged by the parents, often when the children were only infants. But there had to come a point when the couple became aware of the engagement and began to make their plans. I imagine young Joseph. The wedding date is approaching, and he is making preparations. I can see Mary. The date every young lady lives for is just about here. She is so excited as she and her parents make the wedding plans. She and Joseph have such

209

dreams for their lives together. But then, *God messed with their plans!*

It was not in their goals for Mary to become pregnant before their wedding night, and certainly, the idea of becoming pregnant miraculously and giving birth to the Lord Jesus Christ was not the foremost of their thinking. Mary's reaction to the news was one of perplexity. She asks in Luke 1:34, "How shall this be, seeing that I know no man?" Joseph's reaction was a little different. He has a decision to make. Should he believe that Mary has been faithful to him and that she had miraculously become pregnant with the Son of God? Or should he decide to break off the engagement? Of course, you know the rest of the story. They did get married and did give birth to the Messiah, and the rest is history. Let me make three observations based upon this biblical scene.

I. God didn't ask Joseph and Mary he told them.

I do not know any passage where the angel announcing God's plan asked Mary or Joseph if it was acceptable to them. God simply told them his plan and will for their lives. How many of us are doing what we planned on doing when we were in the seventh grade? Most of us aren't doing what we thought we would be doing when we graduated from high school. I have found that the majority of the plans I had as a young person are radically different from what has really come to pass.

Some of the plans have changed because I have changed my decisions and desires. But other plans were changed because of the circumstances beyond my control: *God!* And God has never asked me when he has chosen to put those circumstances into my life. Listen, God has a plan for your life. He made that plan before he created the world. And he has no intention of asking your permission to proceed with his plan. Now you can choose not to obey his will. But you cannot change his will for your life.

As children of God, we attempt to find our way through this maze of experiences known as life, sometimes becoming lost and confused; one thing we must never forget is that God has a plan. Sometimes personal misfortune and tragedy overtake us, and circumstantial ill winds buffet us. When we have reversals in our careers, when sickness and disease attack our bodies, or when the death angel snatches a loved one from us, our faith is sometimes shaken, and we wonder why things happen. But like Joseph and Mary, in all that this maze has to offer, let us never forget that God has a plan.

II. God's plan for Mary and Joseph was not an easy one

Sometimes we think that if we are in the will of God, everything will be a bed of roses and life will be without trial or difficulty. That was not the case for Joseph and Mary. Let's consider this: Why didn't God work it out so the tax was collected either before Joseph and Mary were married or after the Baby was born? He could have done that, couldn't he? I mean, having a woman who was so pregnant that she just barely got to Bethlehem before she had the baby travel by foot, camel, or donkey would not have been easy! Surely

God could have worked things out better than that. The baby was born in a manger because there was no room in the inn. Again, I can see the young couple's frustration as, after traveling so far, Mary is exhausted ready to deliver, and they can't find any place comfortable even to take her! Now, God is a sovereign God. He is able to do anything he wills. He obviously has willed that there is no room in the inn! He isn't making it easy for them, even though they are obeying the will of God for their lives.

Why were they forced to flee Bethlehem to Egypt because of the threat of King Herod? Again, we can see the hand of God at work because he warned them of the danger so they could flee. Whey didn't he just make the king's heart soften so they wouldn't have to flee at all? Especially since all the babies two years old and younger were killed by Herod's men after Mary and Joseph were gone. The Baby was about two years old when they went to Egypt. And that would not have been an easy trip to make! Then, after all of this, somewhere between when Joseph took his family back to Nazareth, and when Jesus became thirty years old, Joseph died. Jesus had become the head of the home, taking care of his mother and his half-brothers and -sisters. We make a terrible error in our concept of Christianity when we believe that God makes life easy when we are in his will and that the easy way is God's way.

Take for instance Jesus's message about two roads: (A) The broad and easy way that almost everyone takes is the way that leads to destruction. (B) The straight, narrow, and more difficult way is the way that leads to eternal life.

When we choose that way that looks the easiest, we aren't necessarily choosing the way that is the will of God! Christ chose a path that led to the cross. Paul chose a path that led to imprisonment and execution. Both chose paths that were in the plan of God for them! God does not promise us an easy trip. He promises to be with us as we take it. The word says, "When thou passest through the waters, I will be with thee, and through the rivers, they shall not overflow thee: when thou walkest through the fire thou shalt not be burned; neither shall the flame kindle upon thee." God assures us of his presence in the midst of troubles. Although God does not remove our troubles from us because God has control of them, God does not leave us alone to withstand them.

III. Though things were differenct, God did bless

I see it through two thoughts: (1) they wondered at the child as he grew. Look at these verses in Luke 2:52 "And Jesus increased in wisdom and stature, and in favor with God and man." Luke 2:49–51 "and he said unto them, how is it that you sought me? Did you not know that I must be about my father's business? And they understood not the saying which he spake unto them. And as he went down with them, and came to Nazareth, and was subject unto them: but his mother kept all these sayings in her heart." Luke 2:40 "And the child grew, and waxed strong in spirit, filled with wisdom; and the grace of God was upon him." Luke 2:33 "And Joseph and his mother marveled at those things which were spoke of him." It must have been a joy to raise Christ as he grew up. That would have been a blessing in itself. But let's look at the big picture: Christ grew to be a blessing to the whole world. Any parent is blessed when their child grows up to be a person of influence and importance in the world. More parents are blessed if their child grows up to do something good for mankind. I realize Joseph was gone by this time. But can you imagine the blessing Mary must have experienced when her firstborn son, Jesus Christ, rose victorious over death and the grave? Can you imagine what she must have felt like as she watched him ascend visibly, bodily into heaven! Can you imagine the excitement in her soul when she realized that her son had opened the door to heaven for all who would accept him as savior?

God's plan for our lives is not an easy one. But it is a plan that will lead to our being a blessing to many. Even if his plan is an early death. He is going to use that in some way ultimately to bring more people to a saving knowledge of the truth. God's plan for Fanny Crosby was that a doctor would give her the wrong medicine when she was a baby, resulting in her blindness. Rather than growing up bitter, Fanny Crosby used her condition to make her more spiritually sensitive; she wrote two of her most beautiful hymns we know: "Blessed Assurance"and "All the way my Savior leads me." "

God used the death of H. G. Spafford's children to inspire him to write one of our favorite hymns. Spafford's wife and children were on a ship to England, and he was going to join them there in a short time. However, the ship with his family on board sank. His wife was saved, but his children all died. Back home, Spafford awaited news as to the fate of his family, and when it finally came, it was a telegram from his wife simply saying, "Saved, Alone." Spafford, while mourning their deaths, wrote these words: "When peace like a river attendeth my way, when sorrow like sea billows roll. Whatever my lot thou hast taught me to say, It is well; it is well with my soul."

God didn't ask Spaffford if it was OK to make that part of his plan for him. And I am sure Spafford didn't plan it for himself. But as difficult as God's plan was, it has resulted in something that has blessed countless numbers of suffering souls since it was written.

I'm so glad that God has a plan for our lives. And what fascinates me about God's plan is that God is able to take the evil that people design for our undoing and downfall and turn it around so that it works for our good. I'm so glad that God has a plan for our lives. For Jesus came in accordance with God's plan. When Satan decided that he would hold humanity captive, God had a plan for our redemption. Wrapped in love, grace, and truth, God stepped across time and was born as a baby in Bethlehem. He grew into a man who refused to compromise with wrong, and when Satan and the forces of evil decided that they would destroy him with the worst possible death they knew—death on a cross—Jesus declared that he would take that cross that degraded others and use it as the pledge for our redemption. For he said: "And I, If I be lifted up from the earth, I'll draw all men unto me." Lift him up! Lift him up! Life him up!

Sermons on the
Celebration of Lent/Easter

———— ∝ ————

While suffering is a universal human experience, the redemptive suffering of the oppressed gives distinctive meaning to the Lent and Easter seasons in the black church. The themes of despair and joy, life out of death, and God's ultimate victory are especially relevant to the spiritual needs of black Christians. For example, Good Friday observances rehearse the agony and pain of Jesus on the cross through the preaching of the seven last words but also celebrate the faith and confidence that God will deliver Jesus. Rather than focus only on the agony of the cross and death of Jesus, the black church anticipates the coming victory. This anticipation of victory over and above the present pain has been one of the keys to survival for black people. This kind of faith finds joyous expression during the Easter season.

Our journey during Lent and Easter exemplifies renewal and growth that are at the heart of the spiritual metamorphosis that must take place in the lives of penitent Christians. On the personal level, real spiritual renewal comes about through the recognition and acknowledgement of sin and death in one's life. Then through confession and repentance one can move from death into new life in Christ.

Through these messages, let's not dismiss the presence of sin and transgression but celebrate that when it's placed under the authority and mercy of God, hope provides the strength to endure. Let's celebrate that a resurrected people exist because of a resurrected Christ.

WHAT I LEARNED FROM A THIEF

—⤫—

Luke 23:42–43 (NKJV)

*"Then he said to Jesus, Lord, remember
me when you come into your kingdom. And
Jesus said to him, Assuredly, I say to you,
today, you will be with me in Paradise."*

There is a lesson to be learned from this particular scene at Calvary. It is a lesson of confession and repentance as the requirements for Eternal Life. Just think with me for a moment on the event of two thieves before Jesus on the cross and one of them turns to Jesus and says, "Remember me when you come into your kingdom." Everybody needs a friend. Jesus began this long campaign against Satan back at Bethlehem and now begins his final scene with only one friend. You can imagine how Jesus must have felt to have been betrayed, denied, and covered up. Have you ever felt all by yourself, as if there was nobody to help? I have seen the awful look upon the face of people being wheeled toward the operating room, out of sight of family and friends. There are times of great testing that make us feel so by ourselves, so beyond the help of all who are deeply and sincerely interested in us. A major examination, a long journey alone, a decision you must make and with no one to help you, that terrible moment when the realization first gets through the shock that someone you love very dearly is dead and gone. It's always good to have someone to wish us well, someone who will wave to us as we take a plane or ship or train someplace, or to be so near that they can put their hands on our shoulders and say, "I know how you feel! I can sympathize with you because I've been there."

But Jesus seems not to even have that. If you read carefully the seven last words, you will note the sorrow of a weeping mother whose words could not soothe the pain and agony of being alone. It was the emptiness, the forsakers, the abandonment, the estrangement and the awesome numbing experience Jesus passed through at Calvary. He was truly a man of sorrows and acquainted with grief. It will not be possible for the human mind to imagine the tortured and troubled regions of lostness and loneliness Jesus went through on Calvary. He had no earthly friends left, at least none on record who would say a word on his behalf. He was truly a wounded Savior whom "the Lord hath laid on him the iniquity of us all."

There seemed to be no friend on earth, not even a friend in Heaven, but the Lord at Calvary met a newfound friend. It was one of the dying thieves who reached out to a dying savior and poured on the suffering Lord the balm and oil of his own praise and reverence. He wasn't much—a convicted criminal, a condemned revolutionary, or worse, a highway robber who had been tried and found guilty. And Jesus was condemned in his death with the transgressors. But he was the only friend who spoke a word in his behalf while he fought a lonely battle with the assembled armies of Satan and death and hell. There were three crosses on that lonely bloodstained hill outside Jerusalem's gate. Two who were below society's standards of decency and one who was above society's standards died on the same hill.

There was a division on the hill that Friday. One of the thieves joined the crowd who hounded the Savior with their its mockery. Perhaps he thought if he joined the jeering crowd he would show his toughness. He had started the race with a sneer on his face, and he thought to end it with a curse on his lips. One thief died unforgiven and the other taught us a lesson in confession and repentance. This thief who did not join the crowd taught us that we can be forgiven of our sins if we ask for it in Jesus's name. He turned to the other thief and said, "Don't you fear God? This is not a time to be cursing and ranting? You are in the same condemnation and we are receiving just punishment for our sins, but this man has done nothing wrong."

I found this to be a statement of simple justice and fair play. While the courts and religious leaders found condemnation in an honest life. A thief on the cross, condemned, a robber showed more justice and honesty than they. One does not have to be a leader to be just, but one has to admit that Jesus Christ has done no harm to the world.

Millions have found in him a better life because they put their faith in him. Drunkards have put down their bottles, gamblers have put aside their dice and cards, dope addicts have thrown away their needles. Jesus has done nothing wrong to the world. The more I read and study the life of Jesus, I see he is more than just a good man. Someone wrote, "He's the fairest of ten thousand to my soul." But he's more than that. Jesus is more than the pioneer of our faith. He is more than the fairest flower of our humanity.

The dying thief saw more in the dying Savior than a good man as the haze of heat, agony, and pain embraced him in the arms of death. The dying thief saw a king climbing great red stairs of pain toward a coronation. He saw a king with blood marks reaching forth to take the scepter of the world in his nail-pierced hand. He saw the Prince of Glory approaching the moment of his enthronement. When he turned to the Lord, he saw the bright and morning star in life's darkest night. He saw a road marker—the road that would take him to God. The thief said, "Lord, remember me when you come into your kingdom."

It is also to be remarked that the thief's conversion took place before the supernatural phenomena of that day. He cried, "Lord, remember me" before the hours of darkness, before the triumphant cry "It is finished," before the rending of the temple veil, before the quaking of the earth and the shivering of the rocks, before the centurion's confession: "Truly this was the Son of God." God purposely set his conversion before these things so that his sovereign grace might be magnified and his sovereign power acknowledged. God designedly chose to save this thief under the most unfavorable circumstances that no flesh should glory in his presence. God deliberately arranged this combination of unpropitious conditions and surroundings to teach us that "Salvation is of the Lord," to teach us not to magnify human instrumentality above Divine agency, to teach us that every genuine conversion is the direct product of the supernatural operation of the Holy Spirit.

The thief asked for one more chance. I learned that from the thief. I don't know of any cry more appropriate for us than the cry for one more chance. The world has failed so tragically; Lord, we need one more chance. Black people starting out after slavery had become so brutalized and purposeless, one more chance we needed from the Lord, and thank God for another chance to make a difference in the world. We have to be abased before we can be exalted. We have to be stripped of the filthy rags of our self-righteousness before we are ready for the garments of salvation. We have to come to God as beggars, empty-handed, before we can receive the gift of eternal life. We have to take the place of lost sinners before him if we could be saved.

The cry of the thief: "Lord, remember me when you come into your kingdom." He looked away from the present to the future. He saw beyond the sufferings, the glory. Over the cross, the eye of faith detected a crown. And in this he was before the Apostles, for unbelief had closed their eyes. Yes, he looked beyond the first Advent in shame, to the second advent in power and majesty. I don't think there is a better prayer we can pray today, no more fitting plea than to ask the Lord to remember us.

The thief asked a question, and Jesus had the answer. I like what Jesus had to answer to the dying thief. The Lord must have felt so encouraged because here was one who saw something of what it was all about and who was proof of his word: "And I, if I be lifted up from the earth, I'll draw all men unto me." These are the thoughts and words of a dying man. "Lord, remember me," He said. "Today, I can get you home myself. You've never been to my home; I'll get you there myself. In my Father's house are many mansions; if it were not so, I would have told you. I go to prepare a place for you, yet when he adds, I will come again he does not say, and conduct you unto the Father's house, but I will get you home myself. I will make sure your passport is stamped, so that you will get home this day … this hour … this moment …"

THE REALITY OF THE RESURRECTION

———✄———

Mark 16:6–7 (NIV)

"Don't be alarmed, he said. You are looking for Jesus the Nazarene, who was crucified. He has risen! He is not here. See the place where they laid him. But go, tell his disciples and Peter, He is going ahead of you into Galilee. There you shall see him, just as he told you."

The basic statement of the Christian faith is that Jesus Christ is risen! Mary Magdalene, Mary the mother of Jesus, and Salome are doubters and worriers. After the Sabbath day has passed, they take the responsibility to minister to Jesus one more time by anointing his head with spices that will counter the smell of physical decomposition. Despite their devotion, they expect his death to be permanent. They also worry all the way to the tomb, asking each other, "Who will roll away the stone from the door of the tomb for us?" Obviously, their expectations do not include a miracle. Otherwise, they would never have approached the tomb with their heads down, a sign of doubt and worry as well as grief.

Physical proof of the Resurrection begins to unfold before their eyes when they look up to see that the massive stone has been rolled away. Entering the tomb, they find it empty except for a young man clothed in a long, white robe sitting on the right side of the stone bench where Jesus's body had been. Through their alarm, they hear him speak the fact that they are seeking Jesus of Nazareth who was crucified but now is risen. The tomb is empty, and they can see for themselves the empty place where Jesus lay.

The physical facts of the Resurrection are in. Jesus, who was crucified on Friday, is gone from the tomb on Sunday. Three women who expected to find a decomposing body in a tomb sealed by a stone too heavy for them to move are eyewitnesses to an empty tomb, an empty bench, and an empty shroud.

The resurrection is something all of us ought to think about, and when we think about it, our thoughts always turn around the great promises:

> "I go to prepare a place for you, that where I am there you may be also."

> "Because I live you shall live also."

> "Those who believe in Me though they are dead, yet shall they live…"

> "Lo, I am with you always."

In the challenges and chances of life, we hold on to the promises that enable us to look beyond the present sufferings, sorrow, and calamity and give us strength to make our way through with his companionship.

Easter is the "main event" of Christianity. It is the victory of Easter that helps us move beyond our sufferings and the inevitable questions, "Why? Why did this happen to me? Why did this happen to mine?" We move beyond that because of the Resurrection to more important questions: "How? How can I face this pain? How can I handle this loss, this challenge, this hurt? How can I turn this pain into a new purpose?" Only the Resurrection can provide us with the capacity to do that. Let us look at three implications of Christ's death and resurrection on our behalf.

I. The Risen Christ enables us to face the reality of our sins.

The word affirms very emphatically that "all have sinned and come short of the glory of God" (Romans 3:23). I would be the first to acknowledge that there is not one of us who is all bad. And at the same time none of us is all good. In times like these, we need a savior. The prophet Isaiah spoke these words many years ago. Here is the way he described Jesus: "But he was wounded for our transgressions, He was crushed for our iniquities; the punishment that brought us peace was upon him, and by his wounds we are healed. We all, like sheep, have gone astray, each of us has turned to his own way, and the Lord has laid on him the iniquity of us all" (Isaiah 53:5, 6).

Jesus followed through using this same shepherd metaphor of shepherd and sheep, stating that the good shepherd cares for his sheep, the good shepherd knows his sheep by name, and the sheep know the voice of the good shepherd. He went on to say: "I am the good shepherd: I know my sheep and my sheep know me, just as my father knows me and I know the father and I lay down my life for the sheep."

Because of what Jesus Christ did for you on the cross, you are free to come to him in an honest, open confession of sin and find his forgiveness because he bore your sins on that cross in order to set you free from sin. Years later, the Apostle John stated one the greatest spiritual facts: "If we confess our sins, he is just and willing to forgive us" (I John 1:9).

II. The Risen Christ enables us to face the reality of our suffering.

One of the dangers of Easter is that we sometimes sugarcoat the reality of human suffering. We want to deny the holocaust we have perpetrated on each other. We want to run away from the reality of our own human pain. Remember every pain you feel, Jesus feels too. He has been there, where you and I have been. Listen again to the words of the Prophet Isaiah: "He was despised and rejected by men, a man of sorrows, and familiar with suffering. ... Surely he took up our infirmities and carried our sorrows" (Isaiah 53:3, 4).

Nicholas Wolterstorff, in his book titled *Lament for a Son*, says, "'Put your hand into my wounds,' said the risen Christ to Thomas, 'and you will know who I am.'" The wounds of Christ are his identity. They tell us who he is. He did not lose them. They went down into the grave with him and they came up with him—visible, tangible, palpable. Rising did not remove them. He who broke the bonds of death kept his wounds.

There's an ancient legend that recounts how the devil tried to get into heaven by pretending to be the risen Christ. The devil, being the master of disguises, took with him a contingent of demons made up as angels of light and shouted at the gates of heaven, "Lift up your heads, O ye gates, be lift up, ye everlasting doors; and the King of glory shall come in." The angels looked down on what they thought was their king returning in triumph from the dead. They shouted back the refrain from the psalm, "Who is this King of glory?" Then the devil made a fatal mistake. In every particular, save one, he was just like Christ. When the angels in heaven thundered, "Who is this King of glory?" the devil opened his arms and said, "I am." In that act of arrogance, he showed the angels his outstretched palms. There were no wound marks from the nails. With that, the angels saw through his disguise and refused to let the impostor in. Don't ever forget those nailpierced hands. He has been there. He knows what it is to suffer. This God you love and worship is not remote from our human condition. His hands bear the scars as a sign of suffering that equals and exceeds the most you and I will ever bear.

III. The Risen Christ enables us to face the reality of our loneliness with confidence.

Our Lord always goes before us. "Jesus is going ahead of you into Galilee. You will see him there." The fact that he goes before us, preparing the way, gives us great confidence. When the son of William Sloane Coffin, the distinguished former pastor of Riverside Church, New York, was killed in an automobile accident, Coffin preached a sermon with this title: My Son Beat Me to the Grave. How could he preach a sermon in that context? I can tell you how. He was and is confident in the resurrection. Our Lord goes ahead of us and promises that we shall see him there. In fact, we are promised in the Bible that we shall see him face-to-face. He stands with us and goes ahead of us in our suffering. He has gone before us in death, and the Resurrection assures us of victory. When Moses and the children of Israel faced the trackless waste of the desert wilderness, God went before them by day in a pillar of cloud, and by night he stayed among them with a flaming fire. Through years of faithfulness and unfaithfulness, through good times and exile and wars and calamities of every kind that one can only imagine, God always went before his people wherever they were, whatever their needs, dispatching his prophets among them to tell them the truth and consequences of disobedience.

God had gone before the women rushing to the tomb to roll the stone away. God is always and forever going before us—not only to prepare the way but to sustain us in the way we should walk.

One of the most poignant moments I ever experience is when I stand by a gravesite of a veteran who is being accorded the final salute. There is a volley of shots and then "Taps" is played. A story is told that a soldier made an unusual request in writing to the military: "When I die," he wrote, "do not sound 'Taps' over my grave, but reveille, the morning call, the summons to rise."

He could make his request with confidence because he knew our Savior had gone before him—not only in death but in Resurrection. There is no place that we can go that he has not been; there is no place that we need to go that he has not been before. We are comforted this Easter because our Lord always keeps his promises. We are confident this Easter because he always goes before us. We are confident this Easter because we can stand up and be counted and can be heard telling the story.

We keep misplacing our hopes in human structures as if we have not known the Resurrection reality. We find ourselves clinging to the way things have always been. We look at the world around us and respond with anger and despair, as if Christ did not die to make all things new. We spend much of our time in complaint instead of proclamation. Someone has said that there are more people living today in the despair and darkness of dark Saturday than have ever lived in the drama of Friday or the victory of Easter. You see Saturday's children are people living in a kind of empty ritual dance toward death with a despair that grips their hearts in a godless world. Now that's hopelessness, meaningless, alienation. But I urge you today that you can be transformed by the power of Jesus Christ. If you happen to be a "Saturday's child," you can join a group that we call "Sunday's children." Without the resurrection, we are all Saturday's children. But because of what Jesus Christ has done for us, you and I are free to call ourselves "Sunday's children."

There's something about Sunday that is different from any day of the week. And if a person starts hanging around church enough they will start to miss it when they are not here. People love to linger and hang around the church on Sundays. But let's look at the text: Mary and the other women came to the tomb while it was still dark and saw the stone rolled away. In the Easter story recorded in John's gospel, it says when Mary came to the tomb and found the stone rolled away she ran to tell Peter and John. They ran back to the tomb and left, but Mary kept lingering. Because she kept lingering, she heard a voice they didn't hear. Jesus called her by name. Because she kept lingering, she saw what they didn't see. She saw Jesus, her resurrected Lord. Because she lingered, she has the distinction of being the first person to see Jesus in the glory of his resurrection.

I'm trying to tell you that if you linger around here a while, you may run into Jesus. You never know what blessing God has waiting for you. Lingering love may seem like wasted love and energy. But the lesson of Mary Magdalene's example is that lingering love is rewarded. If we stay when others leave, keep going when others stop, draw near when others draw away, are faithful when others desert, live right when others compromise, stay on our knees when others give up, keep loving when others lose patience, believe when others doubt, we shall see Jesus in his glory.

Across the ages his promise comes to those who are possessed with a lingering love: "Be faithful unto death, and I will give you the crown of life."

A LIFE-CHANGING WALK

——————⊂✕⊃——————

Luke 24:15 (NIV)

"As they talked and discussed these things with each other, Jesus himself came up and walked along with them."

As we celebrated Jesus's entrance into Jerusalem on Palm Sunday, we saw in text how Jesus had the courage and determination and the commitment to ride into a city that he knew would be his suffering and death. In Jerusalem they ridiculed him and his disciples abandoned him. He would be nailed to a cruel cross. He would have to give himself over to death, but he rode into Jerusalem anyway. There's a message in that for us today, and it is that there comes a time in all of our lives when we must go to some places that we don't really want to go. Because there are some painful experiences that one has to endure. Jesus had to go through some painful experiences, having gone to Jerusalem. But today, Resurrection Day, we find Jesus walking away from Jerusalem. He is walking away from his place of persecution and suffering. He has conquered the stone that was put in front of his tomb. He is free today, and he is walking away.

On this Resurrection Sunday, I have come to proclaim that you may have to go through Jerusalem, but you can experience a life-changing walk by walking away from Jerusalem. Jerusalem is not a place of permanence. Jerusalem is not your life sentence. You can walk away from Jerusalem. You may have been in Jerusalem last week, but today, this is your life-changing walk.

I believe somebody here has had a life-changing walk because you were supposed to be dead from that gunshot wound or seriously wounded from that physical attack or burned up in that fire that should have consumed your life— you walked away from an accident in which the car was totaled. But you have barely a scratch on you. Somebody knows the joy of a life-changing walk because you had chemotherapy that if you had not received it, you would be dead, but you had a life-changing walk and you were delivered and set free. And on this Resurrection Sunday, the good news is, this is your day! You are experiencing a life-changing walk.

No, walking away is not just a physical walk. You can be in a wheelchair and walk away. You see, walking away is mental, emotional, and spiritual advancement. To have a life- changing walk means you are able to survive to carry on, to move away from, to overcome, and to prevail. God will grant you the power to get up after you've taken a hard fall. God will grant you the power to succeed after a major failure. God will give you the power to reclaim what you lost, to pick up the pieces and succeed. Some of you are here today and clothed in your right minds because you have had a life-changing walk. Some of you are here today and think you are doing all right. You think because you have on new shoes and new outfits that all is well. But I want to tell you that if you are still hung up on your past experiences, of drugs, alcohol, and chain smoking, I want you to know that you need to get busy and have a life-changing walk. You don't have to stay there. This is the day to have your life-changing walk.

First, this story reveals how two men had a life changing walk when they had a Jesus encounter.. You have to understand that, like Jesus, they were walking away from Jerusalem. Now they had not been persecuted there, nor had they been executed. But you can see from their conversation that their hopes and been dashed with the crucifixion of Jesus. So Jerusalem had been a place of suffering and loss for them too. And as the two men were walking from Jerusalem, the Bible says that Jesus came upon them, but they were so blinded by their preoccupation with the death of Jesus that the resurrection of Jesus almost escaped them. Do you want to be like that? The Bible says that Jesus came near them, but their eyes kept them from recognizing him. They were so wrapped up in their losses. They were so wrapped up in their sadness that they could not see the miracle in their midst.

On the road from Jerusalem, Jesus was revealing himself in all of his splendor, but their fleshly nature, their lack of spiritual discernment, prevented them from seeing the gift of God that was in their midst. These two men were so obsessed with talking *about* Jesus that they did not recognize that they were talking *to* Jesus. They were focused on losing him that they could not see that he was right by their side. Somebody needs to know today that Jesus is right by your side. Don't you miss him! Somebody needs to know that when you are distressed, when you are feeling forsaken, he is right by your side. When you are trying to find him in the midst of your losses and grief, he is right by your side. When your enemies are wreaking havoc in your life and you're looking all around for him, open your eyes and you will find him right by your side. When things fall apart and families fall apart, relationships fall apart, you don't have to fall apart, because he is right by your side.

That's what the message of Resurrection Day is. He is not dead. He is not even far off. He has not forsaken you. He is right by your side. And I know there is somebody here today saying, "Yeah, but I don't feel him." And I just want you to know that sometimes it is hard to recognize Jesus when your eyes are blinded by tears and sorrow. When you have been disappointed and hurt, it is hard to see him. When the storms of life are raging, it's hard to connect. But I want you to know today if you would just keep your eyes on Him, just keep trying to find Him, if you just turn to Him in faith, you will receive the same divine revelation the disciples received as they walked away from Jerusalem.

Second, I believe that Resurrection Sunday is about Divine Revelation.. I believe that divine revelation is the order of the day. There is somebody here today who hasn't been to church in a long time, and you need a Jesus encounter. Some in here today are still in Jerusalem. And you still have not received divine revelation. And others are on the road coming from Jerusalem. They have been delivered, but they are still so upset, still so mad, still so busy feeling sorry for themselves that they have not received the resurrection revelation. You have on new shoes, but you don't have revelation. You've got a dance and a shout, but you don't have revelation. You have a position and prestige, but you don't have revelation. You know that before anything else and above all else, you don't need another dress. You don't need another car or another piece of furniture. What you need is divine revelation. You need a Jesus encounter that will change your life. You need divine revelation.

What is divine revelation? Divine revelation is God's deliberate disclosure to God's people of the true knowledge of God's self and God's purposes and God's action on our behalf. Divine revelation is a God encounter in which God imparts God's wisdom and God's understanding to be a believer in such a way that gives strength and power and hope for the journey. Divine revelation is seeing God in all of God's truth, and it is seeing the hand of God moving in your life when all hell has broken loose.

I want you to know today that you need to seek divine revelation, because I have found out that divine revelation can change your life. Divine revelation will give you the courage to do what you've been afraid to do in the past. It will give clarity and purpose to your suffering. We need to open up our hearts and minds on this life-changing walk and receive divine revelation. I believe that if you can get revelation, you will be able to get some peace. If you can get revelation, you can get your joy back. If you can get some revelation, you can start loving yourself again. I promise you that if you get divine revelation, you will start treating your family right. It can bless your marriage. It can bless your home environment.

Notice in verse 17, a question Jesus asked them as they were walking along. "What are you two discussing as you walk from Jerusalem?" Now in this text he used the Greek word *Peritonea*, which means "to walk around, to live, or to conduct one's life." So when Jesus is speaking to them, he's asking them, "What are you walking around? What have you discovered as you proceeded as you are walking away, as you are conducting your life after Jerusalem? What are you devoting your attention to as you walk away?" They talk about what they perceive as the reality of the moment. They lament what has happened in Jerusalem. But at that moment, Jesus begins to teach them and impart wisdom into their lives— the wisdom that they need to perceive things correctly. And Jesus said to them, "Don't you remember what the prophets declared?" And Jesus said to them, "You must not be fooled by the apparent hopelessness of the situation. For you see, the prophet said that Christ had to suffer these things to enter into his glory." And the words that Jesus declared are the words that Jesus still declares to us today. Jesus had to go through Jerusalem so that Jesus could enter into his glory.

Finally, because Jesus walked away and walked into his glory, so we too can have a life changing walk and proceed into the Glory of God.. So what is Jesus saying to you? Jesus had to go through Jerusalem so that Jesus could enter into his glory. I know you have had some hard times. I know that you feel empty inside. I know right now that you're overwhelmed by life's circumstances, but understand this one thing: you're just passing through Jerusalem. You can have a life-changing walk today into the Glory of God. You understand today that this life-changing walk is about more than going through Jerusalem, but it's a life-changing walk into the greatness and the majesty of God. You can walk away from financial setbacks right into his glory. The sickness you are going through is nothing more than a Jerusalem experience. When you have been delivered from Jerusalem, there is no place to go but to the glory of God.

I don't know about you this Resurrection morning, but I intend to wallow in his splendor. I intend to live in the spectacular light of the living God. I am happy today that I had a life-changing walk. When you have that life-changing walk, you walk away from tradition. You walk away from suffering and hurts. You walk away from the loads that you have to bear.

I'm walking away into the glory of God. Who is ready to leave their past behind? Who is ready to put their future into the hands of God. Walk into your glory! Walk into your freedom! Walk into your deliverance! I'm leaving my old ways behind and walking into a bright future God has planned for me.

Going from Religion to Relationship with Christ

———— ⌒✕ ————

Luke 24:1–9

There is a book titled More Jesus, Less Religion written by Stephen Aterburn and Jack Felton. It is a work that deals with the reality of knowing the difference between having a relationship with God and having a religion. What these authors try and make clear is that the church has produced more agnostics and atheists than any other false teaching is the misconception that being religious will keep you from having to deal with the vicissitudes of life. That somehow good religion will anesthetize you from anguish and free you from falling. That somehow, if you've got good enough religion, you won't have to cry sometimes. That somehow, if you got good enough religion, every day will be smooth sailing.

But I've found out that religion is the reason some of us are about to lose our minds. Religion is why we are divided by denominations and dogma. Religion is why Sunday morning is still the most segregated hour in America. Religion is why many of us go to church until trouble arises and then we run away from God.

The truth of the matter is, there is a difference between being religious and having a relationship with God. There's a difference between going to church and being the church. There's a difference between joining a church and joining Christ's disciples. There's a difference between quoting the Bible and living the Bible. There's a difference between knowing about God and knowing God for yourself. And I don't know about you, but I've gone through too much hell, I've been through too many difficult things to fool around with pitiful programs, tired traditions, and silly ceremonies. I came this morning to celebrate the Lord Jesus Christ and to say I need more Jesus and less religion. I believe our text is tailored to teach us that trite traditions and regimented religiosity just won't cut it. We need more Jesus and less religion.

Well, you may be wondering how that's in the text. You know this story all too well. This is the story of Mary and the other women running to the grave of Jesus that first Resurrection morning. They hadn't been able to embalm him on Friday when they gave his body to Joseph of Arimathea. They had put him in the grave right before six o'clock and then the Sabbath began. So they could not go on Saturday to embalm his body with spices, so they went early Sunday morning. They went because they wanted to prepare his body. They went doing what they knew to do when someone died. It was their tradition. It was their social, cultural expression of dealing with death—to go to the grave. But when they got there, he was not there.

The First thing I need you to know today is that Religion will take you where Jesus was but seldom where he is.. The scripture says, "Now upon the first day of the week very early in the morning they came unto the sepulchre bringing their spices which they had prepared." Don't get me wrong. Mary came to do the right thing. Mary came to anoint the body of Jesus with spices. Mary came to do what was culturally acceptable, what was religiously right, what was traditionally appropriate. I'm not saying that's wrong because I believe that tradition and religion have their place. But there's a difference between sound traditions and being stuck on traditionalism—those religious notions that time and God's truth have proven to be nonsense.

This is what happens in the text. It would have been fine for Mary and all of the women to go to the grave if Jesus hadn't said in John 2:19, "Destroy this temple, and I'll raise it in three days." It would have been appropriate for them to be at the grave if, in Mark 8:31, Jesus hadn't reminded them that the Son of Man must suffer many things and be rejected by the elders and chief priests and scribes and be killed and after three days rise again. It would have been good for Mary and the women to be at the grave if Jesus hadn't warned them in Matthew 12:48, "For as Jonas was three days and three nights in the whale's belly, so shall the Son of Man be three days and three nights in the heart of the earth." If Jesus had not said all of this, then it would have been all right for Mary to be at the grave ready to anoint his body. But Jesus had already given them truth that suggested showing up for more burial business would not be necessary.

One of the problems with religion is that, in too many cases, just like Mary and the women, it sends us looking for somebody who's not there, and we end up doing stuff we don't need to do because God has already moved on. And that could be what's going on with a lot of our lives right now. We're going through traditions and religiosity, and the Lord has simply moved on. When the Lord moves on, you can go through the motions, but there'll be no miracles. You can try one more time, but there'll be no efficacy. Some of us in here this morning are following traditions and religious stuff that remind us of where Jesus was, but they don't get us to where he is. I want to be where he is. Can I come closer? More Jesus and less religion.

But Second, Religion will not only take you to a grave; it will put you in a grave where there is no Jesus..

It's in the text: "They found the stone rolled away from the sepulchre and they entered in and found not the body of the Lord Jesus." Now look at this. They came to the grave, walked in the grave—no Jesus. But they were in the grave. They were in the grave, but he was not there. A whole lot of us have walked around looking for Jesus, using religion as our road map, and we've ended up in a grave with no Jesus.

How many of you are tired of going to a place where you thought you would find Jesus but you ended up in a grave? I'm going to say something here that would astonish some and anger others, but you need to understand that God is not in every church. I know some of you want to argue that God is omnipresent—meaning God is everywhere. The truth of the matter is God is omnipresent, but there is a difference between the omnipresence of God and manifest presence of God. Do you know there is a difference between God conceptually being everywhere and his shekinah, God's glory being there? I want to go somewhere where I know the Lord is there. When I walk into church, I want to have a God encounter. When I get in church, I need a word from the Lord. I don't want the latest news of the day; I need a word from the Lord.

We can be religious in other ways. In fact, most things that we do in our lives have religious implications because of the God-shaped void in our lives. See, understand why Mary ran. Mary ran because of her need to see Jesus's body because of her love for and devotion to Jesus. She was at the grave because his absence had already created an emptiness in her. We are religious and sometimes it has nothing to do with God; it's because we're trying to fill a void in our life. (Let me make it plain.) Some of us are religious drinkers and religious eaters. Sometimes we want to judge the drinkers, and here we are eating two hoagies and a two-liter Monday through Friday night because we don't have anybody. Pepsi and potato chips have become our best friends. Some of us have made work our religion; we are workaholics. Somebody in here right now, you are making a living but you don't have a life. You're commercialistic and consumeristic. Everything about your outside looks good, but your insides are in a grave and confused, because you're trying to fill the God-shaped void in your life. And now you're in a grave looking for Jesus and you're confused. Have you ever noticed that you keep dating the same person but they just have different names? Every six weeks or so, you've got to kick one out and you let another one in, only to find out it's the same person but with a new name. I'm confused. I think I'm getting ahead, but I'm falling further behind. I'm confused because I go to church, but I don't feel anything. And, the problem is that the shoulders of religion aren't broad enough to carry confusion. Instead of staying on that crazy carousel, it's time to come out of that grave.

But there's good news in the text. **This is my Third point; God will send a message to your grave...** It's in the text. "Behold, two men stood by them in shining garments: And as they were afraid, and bowed down their faces to the earth, they said unto them, Why seek ye the living among the dead? He is not here, but is risen: remember how he spake unto you when he was yet in Galilee, saying, The Son of Man must be delivered into the hands of sinful men, and be crucified, and the third day rise again."

There were two angelic emissaries there to pronounce the good news. God met the grave seekers at their point of need with a message of hope and healing. Because God knows your heart and because God loves you so much, God will send a messenger to bring a word that will lift you out of your grave. God will send a messenger saying, "Why are you seeking the living among the dead? Why do you keep looking for life in all the wrong places? Look, you ought not to be here looking among dead things for living things. But I knew you would be here, so I'm ready to help you out of your grave.

If you'll go over to John 20, we begin to get an understanding of who Jesus is and even of the grace and mercy of Jesus. Because the eleventh verse of John 20 tell us that when Mary looked into the sepulchre, she saw the angels. When Mary looked in, she saw two angels and she was brought back. The gospel will bring you back.

The Scripture says, "And they remembered his words, and returned from the sepulchre, and told all these things unto the eleven, and to all the rest." In other words, they remembered what Jesus had told them. Their grief had clouded their minds. Their religiosity had distorted their reality. But the *word* brought them back. Yes! The angel's words reminded them of what they already knew, and they interpreted this event in their lives in a way that brought fresh revelation.

And so the women received the word. They received the word, and when they received the word, they ran to tell somebody else. And in a real sense, that's what it means to be saved. When you accept the truth of the gospel of Jesus Christ, it gives you new life and makes you want to tell someone else. And I don't know about you, but in the middle of my grave, I got a word from the Lord. In the midst of my pain, I got a word from the Lord. In the midst of my confusion, I got a word from the Lord. And if I can get word from the Lord, then I know that everything is going to be all right. A personal relationship with Jesus does that, not religion.

And to begin the relationship, we've got to believe in the truth of his death, burial, and resurrection. There are few things Christians don't debate across denominations. And those are that Jesus Christ is the Son of God. That he was born of a virgin. That he walked the streets of Jerusalem, healing the sick and raising the dead. That he suffered under

Pontius Pilate. That he took his stand for right and they took his life. That he was the victim of religious intolerance. But that is not the end of the story. Philippians 2 says "God has given him a name that is above every name." Today we celebrate the name of Jesus. Today we trust in the name of Jesus. Today we find salvation in the name of Jesus. Today we declare there is power in the name of Jesus.

I don't care much for religion; I want to have a relationship with Jesus. There are no ifs in my relationship with Christ; there are only affirmations. I can affirm today that he is my rock in a weary land. He is my shelter in the time of storm. He is my deliverer from the strong hand of Satan. He is my key to the gates of glory. He is my help in ages past, my hope for years to come … eternal home

WHAT IS THE STRENGTH OF YOUR LIFE?

———— ⋊ ————

Philippians 4:4–13 (NIV)

*"I can do all things through Him
who gives me strength."*

S ome years ago in the *New York Times* there appeared an article that was both funny and fascinating at the same time. The headline for the story read, "With Lenin's ideas dead, what to do with his body?" The story centered on what to do with the body, the physical remains of Vladimir Lenin, the founder and former leader of Russia from 1917 to 1924.

You may remember that a monarch known as the czar once ruled Russia, and the last of those czars was killed as part of an overthrow of the Russian government led by a group known as the Bolsheviks. Lenin was the leader of that movement and became leader of the country until his death in 1924 at the age of fifty-three. In honor of their fallen leader, the Russian government sealed Lenin's embalmed body in a glass mausoleum so that people could file by his grave and pay their respects.

What a fitting way to revere the man who forged the doctrines the country was run on. For about seventy years the movement started by Lenin resulted in the creation of a political and military superpower known as the Soviet Union. That nation was the rival of the United States for a period of time known as the Cold War. Hostilities between our two countries lasted from the end of World War II until the fall of the Soviet Union on November 9, 1989. That was the day the Berlin Wall that symbolically divided the east from the west was torn down, and that was the day when the great Soviet Empire began to unravel.

Things have changed in the world in the last thirty years. Today, Russia is no longer a communist country. The teachings and speeches of Lenin are no longer being taught in schools or heard on Russian radio and TV. That entire era of Russian history, which they once thought would last for one thousand years, is now slipping into history and obscurity. The only thing that remains in public view that points back to the fall of the czar and the eventual rise of the Soviet Union is the body of Vladimir Lenin that remains on display in its glass mausoleum. That leads to the headline in the *New York Times* that read, "With Lenin's ideas dead, what to do with his body?"

What's interesting about the article was the fact that at the heart of Communism was the principle of atheism, or the denial of the existence of God. Lenin and all of his successors—from Joseph Stalin to Nikita Khrushchev to

Leonid Brezhnev to Mikhail Gorbachev—accepted the idea that God did not exist, that faith was foolishness and that religion was a crutch for the weak. How strange it is that the man who said there is no God is now dead; his ideas are now discarded and a debate going on about what to do with his dead body? Meanwhile, the ideas of Jesus Christ—the one name that Lenin hated more than any other are more popular than ever and there is no debate about what to do with his dead body because three days after his death God raised Jesus from the dead. The Soviet Union has been dismantled but the church of Jesus Christ goes marching on. The words of Karl Marx that were at the heart of Lenin's beliefs are little more than a lesson in nineteenth- and twentieth-century history. Meanwhile, the words of the Bible are printed in every language on earth. Those words are read and cherished by people all over the world.

I mention this news article to you because there are many people who are inclined to put their faith in the ideas and beliefs of men and women just like themselves. Then that person dies or their ideas go out of fashion, and people are left trying to figure out what to believe in next. The lesson from Paul in our text today is for us to put our faith in a person and in principles that have already stood the test of time. Paul tells us not to get caught up in such passing ideologies as communism or socialism or fascism. All of those ideas and their proponents have come and gone. Instead, we should cling to those things that Paul set forth when he was alive. At the heart of Paul's message is this statement: "I can do all things through Christ who gives me strength." That is one of the most important verses in the entire Bible; our strength comes from the Lord. And that is our first point—**Our Strength comes from the Lord..**

You and I can endure the trials and hardships that intrude into our lives—not because we are strong enough to bear them but because our help comes from the Lord. We can walk through the valley of the shadow of death and not be afraid—not because we are in charge but because the Lord is with our strength and we come from the Lord. Today I want to urge you to establish and maintain a close and abiding relationship with God through Jesus Christ so that when your life comes up against the obstacles, setbacks, and challenges that we all must face, you will have one great assurance; all my help comes from the Lord.

Let me take you back to the words of that headline and the two things it points out about the difference between Vladimir Lenin and Jesus Christ. The first thing that article said was, "Lenin's ideas are dead." There is no great mass of people who continue to study and live by his teachings. There is no great mass of people who turn to his writings or speeches when they are trying to figure out how they are going to live their lives each day. Lenin may be a name they know, but it is a message they love and trust and cherish.

Now consider Jesus Christ. For the last two thousand years people have been turning to and praying to and clinging to Jesus as they have sought to make decisions for their lives both great and small. How many times have you heard somebody say they are going to take some problem to the Lord in prayer? How many times have you said that you were waiting for the Lord to show you the way or give you a sign or lead you where he wants you to go? Unlike Lenin, the ideas of Jesus are not dead. They are not the stuff of history; they are a lamp unto my feet and the light unto my path that guides my life every day.

Is there anybody here today who is ashamed to say that you seek to know the will of God by putting your faith in his son, Jesus Christ? Is there anybody here today who is willing to say that you read your Bible because you want your life to be pleasing to God? Is there anybody here today who still believes that the teachings of the Bible are true and relevant and will stand forever? That is where I am today, I say along with Isaiah 40, "The grass withers and the flower fades, but the word of our God shall stand forever." I say along with Paul in Roman 16, "I am not ashamed of the gospel of Jesus Christ; for it is the power of God unto salvation for everyone who believes."

Second, our Strength comes from thinking and doing the gospel.. What philosophy or ideology has captured your attention? If anything has become more important and more informative to you than the gospel of Jesus Christ, you need to listen to Paul today. Paul says, "Whatever is noble, whatever is right, whatever is pure, whatever is lovely, whatever is admirable—if anything is excellent or praiseworthy—think about such things. Whatever you have learned or received or heard from me, or seen in me, put it into practice." The things taught to us from the Bible are not outdated or passé; they may sound a bit old-fashioned, but they have outlived all the shifting philosophies and opinions of people whose names are now little more than footnotes in history.

Think on and do the things taught in scripture. In a world of racism and warfare and gun violence and immorality, think on what is noble and pure and lovely. Our society is overrun with pornography, lust, and sex. People in America spend more money purchasing pornography than they do on all professional sports combined. This is not just a problem for nonbelievers. This is a problem for every church in the country; people are hooked on pornography just like they are hooked on drugs or alcohol or cigarettes. There is only one way to break an addiction, and that is to get the object of that addiction off your mind and concentrate on something else. Paul says, whatever is pure, whatever is lovely, whatever is admirable or praiseworthy, think on and do those things. You cannot watch an X-rated movie while you are thinking on the things of God. You cannot go inside a topless club or watch sex acts on your computer if your mind is stayed on Jesus. Not only are the ideas of Jesus not dead; those ideas still have the power to break the addictions that grip our lives.

You may have been an alcoholic, but today you are free of that addiction by the power of God and by thinking on his word. You may have held racist views in the past but today your whole mind has changed because you thought on the things of God. And that power can work in every area of your life. It can break every addiction that grips us, from the silliest to the most sinister. You may not be addicted to sex or drugs or alcohol, but what about shopping or eating or gossiping or lying or stealing or profanity or procrastinating?

Are there still some chains that bind you? Are there still any habits that you have dragged around for years that continue to grip you to this day?

Paul tells us those things can be broken. Listen to what he says and make these words your own: "I can do all things through Christ who gives me strength." Christ's ideas are not dead and his body is not decaying in some glass-encased mausoleum. His is alive and well today. He has all power in his hands. When you are sick, he has the power to heal you. When you are frightened, he has the power to encourage and comfort you. When you are confused about which way to go in your life, he has the power to guide and direct your thoughts and your steps. You and I can do all things through Christ who gives us strength.

Finally, our Strength comes from our faith and trust in the bible.. The secret to being successful in life is putting your faith in someone whose teachings and values were cherished and trusted by generations of people before you and I came along. The God mentioned in this Bible brought Moses and the people of Israel out of slavery and across the Red Sea. The God mentioned in this Bible cooled the fiery furnace for three Hebrew boys and locked the jaws of lions for Daniel. The God of the Bible is as old as creation itself and as current as the air we breathe right now.

The Bible is important for another reason. It talks about the God who will outlast our lives and serve to inform all the generations that come after us. It is both humorous and tragic when people put their faith in a person whose ideas die soon after their body dies. While I mentioned Vladimir

Lenin to your this morning, there is another person named Charles "Daddy" Grace who started the United House of Prayer for All People in the midst of the Great Depression of the 1930s. His is a story worth telling on a day when we are talking about what is the source of our strength.

Charles "Daddy" Grace taught his followers that he was actually God. He told them that every time the word "grace" appeared in the Bible, it was actually a direct reference to him. He also taught them that he was the incarnation of the Holy Spirit mentioned in the Bible. He even told them, "If you get in trouble with God, Daddy Grace can help you. But if you get in trouble with Daddy Grace, God can't do you any good." All over the country there were people who abandoned the teachings of scripture and put their faith in the teachings of Daddy Grace. That is until a strange thing happened on January 21, 1960, when Daddy Grace died. What do you do when your god dies? Where do you turn when the person you have been turning to has been turned back to the dust?

Our strength does not come from Lenin's tomb, and our strength does not come from dead Daddy Grace. On January 21, 1960, the day Daddy Grace died, the God we serve was still on the throne. He was still sustaining all of creation. He was still hearing and answering prayer. He was still unlocking other people's graves and ushering them into his presence, where they could live forever in a house not made with hands.

Where do you turn for the help you need each day? Make sure it is somebody whose ideas and whose body is not already dead! I found the source of my strength. How about you? My help comes from the Lord who made heaven and earth. He is my rock and my salvation. He is my bridge over troubled waters. He is my strong tower when enemies come against me. He is the joy and the strength of my life. All my help comes from the Lord. His ideas are not dead and his body is not being preserved in a mausoleum.

> I serve a risen Savior; he's in the world today!
>
> I know that he is living, whatever men may say
>
> I see his hand of mercy; I hear his voice of cheer
>
> And just the time I need him, he's always near
>
> He lives! He lives! Christ Jesus lives today
>
> He walks with me, and talks with me along life's narrow way
>
> He lives! He lives! Salvation to impart!
>
> You ask me how I know he lives; he lives within my heart.

REFLECTIONS ON
THE FIFTY YEARS

———— ✕ ————

I would like to look at my spiritual journey and the many stories I can tell of the wondrous grace of God and the many people whose lives met mine, and together we have come a long way together thanking God for the good days, the bad days, the challenges, and the triumphs. This has truly been a sacred journey that has carried me through some wonderful churches where I was privileged to pastor and to serve with some of the faithful colleagues who allowed me to share in their pulpits, and I in turn invited them to share in my ministry and thus this journey has been one I shall always cherish as a pastor/presiding elder in the African Methodist Episcopal Zion Church.

I am reminded that all of us by God's Grace will have journeys in this life we are allowed to take, and some—as I have been privileged to—will come to a moment in their life when they too can look back and see the hand of God moving them on this journey. Such a journey can be a lonesome one or it can't be guided with the hand of God. I am sharing a time in the life of Frederick Buechner's book titled *Sacred*

Journey. It is the story of Buechner's boyhood and some of the events that shaped his life. The clear message of the book is that all of us are on a spiritual journey and that the events of our lives are really the story of the sacred journey we each make. This is how he says it:

> For all the sons and daughters of Eve, it starts with whatever moment it is at which the unthinking and timeless innocence ends, which may be either a dramatic moment or a series of moments so subtle and undramatic that we scarcely recognize them. But one way or another the journey through time starts for us all, and for all of us, too, that journey is in at least one sense the same journey, because it is what is primarily, I think, a journey in search. Each must say for himself what he is searching for, and there will be as many answers as there are searches, but perhaps there are certain general answers that will do for all of us. We search for a self to be. We search for other selves to love. We search for work to do.

When Jesus was a young man, a new prophet arose in Galilee. It was his cousin John who had long ago left his parents' home to become a hermit in the desert. There John preached to the people a message that was likened to the volcanic eruptions that made the region a wasteland. John's message was a call to repent and be ready for that coming judgment.

Then came Jesus down the riverbank to be baptized by his cousin. He came for the same reason as John's converts. He was troubled by the same symptoms that John held before the people, so he joined others going down into the muddy waters of the Jordan to be baptized. The result was a tremendous religious experience that Jesus could not have described except in symbols to his closest followers. It was an inner experience for Jesus. He felt the heavens open, and God spoke to him, saying: **"This is my beloved Son, I am well pleased with you"**

I don't think it's presumptuous to say that many of us have had such a moment. We might experience it in different ways. Some feel the love of God enfolding them, filling them with such a sense of love, joy, and protection that they know they can never be alone again. For others it is a gradual unfolding that one day results in being aware of a commitment they have made.

As we continue the journey, we are always testing that vision. As Jesus tests his vision by identifying with the great heroes of his people's faith, so we test our vision by identifying with the spiritual giants of our lives. If you think about it, you will know that you have engaged in this part of your journey again and again throughout your life. Where did your vision come from? I think back right now and identify persons who helped shape my vision—bishops who were there for me in my beginning, helped me to understand the role of the pastor, ordained me, appointed me to churches:

Bishop Raymond Luther Jones, Bishop William Milton Smith (ordained me deacon and elder), Bishop Herbert Bell Shaw, Bishop Ruben Lee Speaks, Bishop J Clinton Hoggard, Bishop Clinton Rueben Coleman, Bishop George Washington Carver Walker Sr, and presently Bishop George Edward Battle Jr

There were teachers who admired me and believed in me, ministers who opened faith for me, spiritual giants who taught me about prayer. We have all been touched by this great cloud of witnesses. Having loved them and perhaps felt their love for us, we have shaped our vision in certain ways. Because we experience God's love and want to be responsive to it, we shape our lives by the visions God gives us about how we should love and care for the people around us. When the going gets tough, as it does, we return again and again to the source of power that transfigures us and helps us move on. I suggest to you that Jesus's sacred journey and the ones that you and I will take lead at some point to the challenge of a job that must be done. It may be a task to do, a witness to make, a ministry to perform, or a sacrifice to offer. It may be the hardest thing you've ever done. None of us setting out on this journey can escape the demand to act; that at some time will come so that some more ultimate good will result.

My beloved, we are here because we are part of a sacred journey. We may be at different stages in that journey. Some of us find ourselves, regardless of our age, at the opening of that journey—at the farewell to innocence when we first know that God cares about us and we are challenged to accept responsibility in God's name.

Others of us have moved along on our journey and need to test our direction and insights or examine why we are stuck at a particular plateau. Some of us are at the point of knowing God has a particular job for us to do and are fearful about what it will mean if we do it.

I close with a quote from the dean of Black Preachers in America—the late Reverend Dr. Gardner Calvin Taylor— from his book he coauthored with the late Reverend Dr. Samuel DeWitt Proctor titled *We Have This Ministry*:

> **All in all, a summons to the ministry is no light calling. Those of us who have heard the call and have discerned within the voice of God live daily with its profound impact. The work of communicating the gospel requires us to be more than what we are-to exceed who we are. Then by the grace of God we will be delivered of the gospel to a world which is perishing without it.**

BIO OF REVEREND DOCTOR MICHAEL E. ELLIS

———✷———

The Reverend Dr. Michael E. Ellis, is a native of Salisbury North Carolina. Dr. Ellis was educated in the public schools in Salisbury, and graduated from Salisbury High School. Dr. Ellis is a graduate of Livingstone College in Salisbury, N.C. obtaining a Bachelor of Arts in Sociology; and a Master of Divinity Degree from Hood Theological Seminary, Salisbury, N.C.; and the Doctor of Ministry Degree from Drew University.

Dr. Ellis began his ministry in 1969. He was ordained a deacon in 1973 and an Elder in 1974. He served as a pastor in the Western North Carolina Conference; the Western New York Conference; the Tennessee Conference and the New England Conference.

Dr. Ellis is the Presiding Elder of the Greensboro District; Piedmont Episcopal District; and the chair of the Religious/Liberal Studies Department at Livingstone College in Salisbury, NC; Trustee Emeritus at Hood Theological Seminary, Salisbury, NC; retired Naval Reserve Chaplain; a former Adjunct professor of Christian Social Ethics at Boston University School of Theology; a former Division Chair of Liberal Studies at Roxbury Community College, Roxbury, Ma.

Dr. Ellis lives in Colfax, North Carolina, married to Sharlene Renee Ellis; the father of Michael, II and Zoya Ellis, one grand daughter McKenzie.

www.ingramcontent.com/pod-product-compliance
Lightning Source LLC
Chambersburg PA
CBHW032051020426
42335CB00011B/292